Postcolonial Theory and *Avatar*

FILM THEORY IN PRACTICE

Series Editor: Todd McGowan

Postcolonial Theory and *Avatar*

GAUTAM BASU THAKUR

Bloomsbury Academic
An imprint of Bloomsbury Publishing Plc

B L O O M S B U R Y
LONDON • OXFORD • NEW YORK • NEW DELHI • SYDNEY

Bloomsbury Academic
An imprint of Bloomsbury Publishing Inc

1385 Broadway
New York
NY 10018
USA

50 Bedford Square
London
WC1B 3DP
UK

www.bloomsbury.com

First published 2016

Library of Congress Cataloging-in-Publication Data
Basu Thakur, Gautam.
Postcolonial theory and Avatar / Gautam Basu Thakur.
pages cm — (Film theory in practice)
Includes index.
Summary: "An explanation of postcolonial film theory and how it explicates James Cameron's film" — Provided by publisher.
ISBN 978-1-62892-565-4 (hardback) — ISBN 978-1-62892-563-0 (paperback)
1. Avatar (Motion picture : 2009) 2. Postcolonialism and the arts. I. Title.
PN1997.2.A94B37 2015
791.43'72—dc23
2015016807

ISBN: HB: 978-1-6289-2565-4
PB: 978-1-6289-2563-0
ePub: 978-1-6289-2569-2
ePDF: 978-1-6289-2566-1

Series: Film Theory in Practice

Typeset by RefineCatch Limited, Bungay, Suffolk, UK

To Baba

That Midnight's Child who taught me

Marx and introduced me to Freud

(1947–2013)

CONTENTS

ACKNOWLEDGMENTS

This book is presaged by a symbolic murder and underwritten by a real death. I stand inescapably guilty of the first and exist as a soul-sapped survivor of the latter. Writing this book gave me the opportunity to confront my guilt and somewhat mediate my suffering. I thank first he who is already dead. Second, I thank all those who are alive and who surround me and make me feel alive but also remind me constantly of our inevitable being-toward-death.

Then, there are those people in my life without whose presence, help, and good wishes this book could never have been written. First among them is Todd McGowan. I could not have written this book without his inspirational guidance. I have learnt a lot from him as I have also learnt to disagree with him in the last few years; I owe to him more than gratitude. I am indebted to the English department at Boise State University for granting me a course release in spring 2014 for writing the book. Thanks are specifically due to Michelle Payne and the members of the Faculty Affairs Committee. Thanks are also due to the staff at the Boise State's Albertsons's Library; the students in my fall 2014 critical theory class; and, my research intern Ms. Alison Lippincott. I also wish to take this opportunity to thank my colleagues: Dawn Brown, Whitney Douglas, Jeff Westover, and Dora Ramirez for their friendship, and Bruce Ballenger for his advice about writing. Another special thank you is reserved for Pietro Condemi. Pietro sent me two articles published in *JEP-European Journal of Psychoanalysis* on Cameron's film otherwise unavailable in the United States.

For friendship, reading early drafts, and giving useful comments, thanks to Ralph Clare, Rini Bhattacharya Mehta, and Anustup Basu. I learnt a lot from your observations and suggestions for improvement.

Many people have contributed to the development of my thinking on postcolonial theory, its relevance in the global present, and the possible connections between postcolonial theory and Freudian-Lacanian psychoanalysis. I wish to first thank those specters and intellectual giants who have inspired my thinking (still in process) and with whom I have developed long, impending, imaginary conversations. To Hobbes and Burke, Freud and Spivak, Lacan and Žižek, Derrida and Heidegger, Latour and Fanon, and Grosrichard and Bhabha, I tip my hat. Then my good friends, excellent interlocutors, harsh critics, and inspirational teachers: Michael Palencia-Roth, Wail Hassan, Supriya Chaudhuri, Robert Rushing, Lilya Kaganovsky, Prasanta Chakraborty, Meheli Sen, Anindya Sengupta, Franklin Ridgway, Sandeep Banerjee, Paulomi Chakraborty, Santanu Biswas, Arijit Sen, Pinaki De, Anupam Basu, and Lauren Goodlad. My appreciation to Katie Galoff and Mary Al-Sayed at Bloomsbury for their unwavering enthusiasm about the project and for their help whenever I asked.

To my family in India for understanding my inability to call or Skype during the last year, especially my mother Nupur Basu Thakur and my brother Shubham Basu Thakur. Thank you Reshmi Mukherjee for reading the many drafts of this project, and, above all, for patiently listening to and offering incisive criticisms of my cunning and not so cunning plans about interweaving Spivak with Lacan. Finally, I want to tell Rohitashwya thank you for being a part of my life.

Introduction

The postcolonial avatar

The word *avatar* in Bengali is used in two senses. The first, derived directly from Sanskrit, describes a particular figuration—God's descent on earth in human form or *avatar* as incarnation. The second, its secular and colloquial usage, describes a person whose peculiar and flamboyant dispositions, habits, and character traits isolate him or her (generally, him) from the rest of society as someone who looks or behaves strangely. How is this second usage, one that is as common, if not more so, than the first, related to the traditional, religious connotation of the former?

The connection is to be found in the latter's marking out of identity in relation to the common. The secular avatar, like the *avatar* of God Vishnu (who descends to earth in human form), is both similar to, yet different from the rest of humanity as far as each is marked by specific character traits lacking in the multitude. Just as the divine avatar is different from the common people by virtue of its moral uprightness (Rama), physical strength (Varaha), spirituality (Buddha), or intellect (Krishna), the secular avatar is discernible by the peculiarity of his character traits—his idiosyncrasies, sense of fashion, irascible behavior, implausible actions, and so on. The secular sobriquet can thus typify, for instance, the bumbling yet loveable tramp in *City Lights* (1931), the mischievous Willy

Wonka in *Charlie and the Chocolate Factory* (2005), and Malvolio in Shakespeare's *Twelfth Night* (1601) (especially when he is duped into waiting for Olivia wearing "yellow stockings" and "cross garters"). The marginality of these characters qualifies them as suitable candidates for being distinguished by the secular usage of the Bengali word *avatar*. Yet their respective positions on the margins of our imaginary "green worlds" do not dissolve the shadow they cast on the normative world—a world stained by the tramp's unexpected appearance in the opulent opening scene of *City Lights*, or a normative forever haunted by a lowly steward's explosive utterance in *Twelfth Night*: "My masters, are you mad?" These secular avatars—multicolored characters of mortal provenance, these freaks and misfits and outcastes—thus share another similarity with their divine counterparts. They lead the masses toward critically reexamining their so-called normal lives, their picture perfect communities, and their unquestioningly accepted notion of reality.

There is, however, one crucial difference between the divine and the secular avatar. The avatars of Vishnu appear only at times when forces of evil overrun the earth and there is no human solution in sight. Their job during such times of crises is to expunge the evil from the world and restore mankind back onto the path of *dharma*. A chain of causality therefore structures the manifestations of the divine on earth: His appearance is driven by a goal, the fulfillment of which is possible only with His particular skill, which, in turn, constitutively distinguishes Him from the rest. The secular avatar, by contrast, is without a place in the normative, socially contractual space of the collective.

These corresponding and conflicting meanings of the word "avatar" provide a basis for reflecting on the discipline of postcolonial theory and its application to film analysis in the era of globalization and multicultural politics. Postcolonial theory today requires a new avatar that would critically reexamine the undercurrents of new imperial imaginaries in current discourses by adapting itself to and arranging itself against the contours of the colonized past as well as the globalized present. Theorists need to reimagine postcolonial theory to better train its critical lenses on understanding how the mechanism of subject-production has changed in the geopolitical present compared with the colonial past. The new postcolonial avatar needs to function akin to secular avatars, which demand renewed critical investigation.

It must be clarified that this supposed coming to life of postcolonial theory is not coming back to life. It is not reincarnation, but incarnation or arrival in another form and on another stage adjacent to the dead, which is why the term "avatar" is apt. A new postcolonial theory for the twenty-first century must be genuinely new and not just a regurgitation of past critiques if it is to shock the masses out of their deathlike ideological slumber infused by the current form of palliative capitalism.

The problem is that any imagination of a new incarnation of postcolonial theory cannot free itself entirely from Eurocentric habits of thinking. Even the metaphor of the avatars I employ in the opening implies a reconciliation of the divine and the secular that aligns with Western epistemology, especially in the tradition of Hegel. The desire for a new incarnation is itself the product of an essentially European line of critical thinking and this poses the question: Is the incarnation of postcolonial theory itself destined to be Eurocentric?

The answer is "no." But then it is also not the complete answer. For if I hypothetically agree for a moment that my wish is indeed underwritten by a Eurocentric habit of thinking, then that does not disclose anything else than the predicament of the Third World postcolonial theorist. As products of European education, the Third World postcolonial intellectual is structured by and grounded in European Enlightenment epistemology. One cannot question that. But as this current discussion attests, the Third World postcolonial theorist is also keenly aware of the limits of her intellectual grounding. Does that mean postcolonial theorists and the work they do are best defined as perverse: they know it is impossible to transcend Europe as a category of thought, yet in their writings they continue to deplore the stranglehold of Europe on cultural expressions of the non-West? Or are they allowed by the First World academy and its structuring logic of capitalism to be contrarian for the sake of multicultural identity politics? Better still, does the perverse condition of the Third World postcolonialist theorist in the First World academy describe the inherent character of postcolonial theory? I take these issues up for an expanded discussion in the first chapter of this book. Here I want to note briefly that the postcolonial theorist, in being aware of the impossibility of extending a genuine postcolonial critique without first deconstructing her own subject position in the First World academy, often enunciates a most radical gesture—she deracinates herself from her intellectual home! This habit of continually deconstructing every single postcolonial utterance made constitutes the core differential of postcolonial theory as a practice and a philosophical exercise from most other disciplinary practices. Namely, postcolonial theory identifies negativity and split as critical gestures warranted against holistic Eurocentric appropriations of the Other as well as its critique of Europe's appropriations of the Other. My wish to bridge the divine and the secular is therefore not aimed at overcoming the split, but, rather, to illustrate the appearance of the postcolonial in being and practice (or, becoming as practice) as due to that split.

Postcolonial theory, at its best, is in a continuous process of flux and reformation, and this book attempts to embody this process. And it is ironic but fitting that such a theoretical discipline is called on to investigate the phenomenon of globalization, which comes into being through change, uncertainty, and fleeting opportunities.

Globalization promotes a subjectivity that is autonomous, flexible, and capable of expanding into the farthest reaches of the globe. Yet, as Victor Li perceptively observes, this "new" discourse of globalization is neither new nor free from the logic of the capital. The global subject of the West still relies on discourses of enterprise and the othering of the Other for legitimizing its condition of being as did Daniel Defoe's Robinson Crusoe 300 years ago. If anything has changed, it is the new global subject's engagement with the indigenous Other. Unlike Crusoe, whose first reaction on seeing human footsteps on the beach of "his" barren island was that he would now have a servant, recent discourses are extremely cautious in avoiding negative representations of the Other. At times, contemporary discourse goes to the length of even avoiding the Other entirely, as in Robert Zemeckis's *Cast Away* (2000), which shows the Western hero stranded on an uninhabited island without the indigenous Friday who accompanied Crusoe.[1] As a postcolonial theorist, one must remain deeply skeptical of globalization's discourse of all-inclusive sustainable economic development and its reimagination of the subject. Subject-production in globalization remains singularly dependent on strategies of othering the Other, though such acts are cloaked in rhetoric of multicultural tolerant pluralism. What follows is therefore a keenly self-conscious reimagination of the postcolonial disciplinary home for purposes of interrogating the reimagined subject of the West in the global world.

The postcolonial is dead!

Though criticisms of postcolonial theory are as old as the institutionalization of the discipline in the Anglo-American academy, it is only recently that the end of postcolonial theory has been rehearsed into (almost) veridical existence. The catalyst is globalization, especially its productive (rather than prohibitive) form of power and permissive structures of dominance. The West in a global, networked, and hybrid world is not only dependent upon the non-West for most of its daily items of subsistence; it also no longer seeks to marginalize or erase the Other for being different.[2] Rather, driven by the logic of global capital, the postcolonial West in the twenty-first century celebrates difference by actively promoting (up to a point) the uniqueness of all existing worldwide cultures. The Other today is no longer marginalized in our societies and no longer confined to the margins of our texts. Consequently postcolonial theory, with its supposed dependence on the binary of colonizer and colonized, its retrieval of marginalized histories, and its oppositional identity-politics, is no longer relevant to the geopolitical present. The postcolonial is dead.

When a discipline seems to die, this offers an opportunity to examine what constitutes it and to understand it anew. We can specifically diagnose it in order to see if it was sick all along and suffering from congenital defects—riddled by faulty methodology and lack of analytic strength, and surviving only as long as it did by fortuitous chance and planned politicking. The purpose of this book is to take up this line of questioning and to undertake the task of reimagining the postcolonial in a new avatar in order for it to effectively examine the current vagaries of global geopolitics. This will occur in two parts: first, through an overview of postcolonial theory, and second, through employing postcolonial theory to analyze a contemporary film, James Cameron's *Avatar* (2009).

Reinvention of the postcolonial today will, however, require more than vociferously defending its usefulness at a time when some of its old critical coordinates appear to be truly unusable for interrogating globalization as a new avatar of European imperialism. Similarly, the tendency in some of the current debates about the future of the postcolonial, namely to salvage whatever might be deemed advantageous from the dead theoretical apparatus and then to recycle these as postcolonial redux, must be avoided at all costs since this course of action closely symptomizes our late capitalist habit of disposable consumption. Simply put, we cannot upbraid postcolonial theory for failing to effectively engage with twenty-first century capitalism and work at the same time on recycling it into "postcolonial 2.0" pursuant to the logic of the global capital. What we need to do instead is return to the foundations of postcolonial theory, including those judged insufficient to question global capitalism, those purported to be dead, and those considered incompatible with the political goals of postcolonial theory. In pondering the death of and return to the postcolonial I propose we reach into its most darkling inside—into the postcolonial *unheimlich* or uncanny.

The call to defamiliarize the disciplinary home of postcolonial theory is concomitant with a belief that a radical rearrangement of the postcolonial theoretical lens is necessary for interrogating the manifest content of globalization as discourse underwritten by the longstanding credo-narrative of Europe as the universal (or, Europe as the subject and producer of knowledge) versus the Other as particular. As the problem today is not racism or hegemony but racism without racists and hegemony without dominance, the job of the postcolonial theorist is more important.[3] Postcolonial theory needs to continue raising questions about subject-production and knowledge-production, what I am calling here the cultural production of meaning, in Western discourses. This task though is not one of detection, that is of saying Europe is Eurocentric. We know already that the emperor has no clothes and that it is perfectly natural for Europe to be Eurocentric. In fact, as Hamid Dabashi recently remarked, it would only be curious if Europe was to not be Eurocentric.[4] The task, more importantly, is to unravel the concealed processes used for the production of truth under the control of Europe.[5]

Postcolonial theory has not lost its significance in the twenty-first century. This is because the inclusive, non-discriminatory rhetoric of globalization is duplicitous and because racial prejudice and ethnic stereotyping remain present in contemporary discourses. In fact, as is well attested by news around the world, racial profiling of the Other is on the rise. However, unlike in the previous centuries, today it occurs under a vocabulary of self-criticism, white guilt, tolerance, multiculturalism, and inclusive economic growth. Instead of being dead, colonial-era Eurocentrism is enjoying a resurrection today in a new guise. Postcolonial theory must be reimagined to recognize and counter the existence of Eurocentrism beneath the West's politically correct representations of the Other.

In this book, I reimagine postcolonial theory to meet the need for examining the reimagined Eurocentrisms of the present. Robert Young, in arguing for the relevance of postcolonial theory today, notes that it must successfully identify "the hidden rhizomes of colonialism's historical reach" by focusing on the invisible, unseen, and unspoken alongside the "life of residues" and "living remains" of colonial-era Eurocentrism in discourse.[6] In my reimagination, postcolonial critical practice must continue to interrogate the presence-in-absence of marginality (in diverse forms and various figures) in dominant narratives of the West, but it should not stop there. Rather, postcolonial theory needs to extend its analytic scope and contextualize representations of marginality in relation to the ontology of the West. That is, it must extend into the critical practice examining the non-West as paradoxically both constitutive of and disruptive of the West's symbolic identity. The direction of postcolonial analysis accordingly should not be restricted only to studying the processes through which the West represents the non-West and the discourses authorized by such representations. Instead, postcolonial analysis should be directed uniformly at investigating the West's discursive negotiations of the non-West that exists as an irreducible presence and in apposition to the West's fundamental arrangement of its subjective identity.

The structure of the book

The book is divided into two main chapters. The first chapter, "The Postcolonial Avatar: A Brief History of Postcolonial Theory," presents an overview of postcolonial theory. In the context of the current crisis of the discipline, this chapter reimagines and repurposes postcolonial theory by reading it through, and adjacent to, psychoanalytic thought. In a sense, it makes the home of postcolonial theory unhomely (*unheimlich*) by bringing out foreclosed and (im)possible readings through reconsideration of the writings of its three main theorists, namely, Edward Said, Gayatri Chakravorty Spivak, and Homi Bhabha.[7] This chapter balances keeping theory speculative, thereby inviting critical imagination and intellectual contemplation on the part of the reader, while explicating the basic contours of postcolonial theory in a way comprehensible to both the uninitiated as well as mature students of theory.

But why only Said, Spivak, and Bhabha? In focusing on the trio, I am following an established though problematic practice of differentiating between postcolonial theory/theorist and postcolonial criticism/critic. According to Bart Moore-Gilbert, Said, Spivak, and Bhabha belong to the camp of postcolonial theorists, while figures such as Aijaz Ahmad, Abdul JanMohamed, Arif Dirlik, Stephen Sleemon, and Anne McClintock, are in the criticism camp. (One should add Benita Parry's name to this list as well.) He underscores the difference between the two groups by characterizing the work of the theorists as derived from French high theory and identifying those opposed to such derivative analyses as the postcolonial critics. The critics, Moore-Gilbert tells us, are united only by their "shared hostility towards the supposedly reactionary politics of postcolonial theory."[8] Dennis Walder, while following Moore-Gilbert's schema of differentiating the theorists from the critics, proposes another way to differentiate between the theorists and the critics. He says that Ahmad and Parry are part of the *materialist* wing of postcolonial theory, while Spivak, Said, and Bhabha belong to the *textualist* wing.[9] In other words, and I will revisit this argument in some detail in chapter one, the work of the postcolonial theorists focuses mainly on textual or discourse analysis while that of the postcolonial critics on the material conditions emerging from colonial rule and affecting the production, circulation, and dissemination of colonial discourse.

I do not fully endorse Moore-Gilbert's strict categorization. Postcolonial theory and postcolonial criticism share mutual concerns, and it is also a futile exercise to delimit the works of theorists such as Spivak as one or the other. In any case, considering the difficulty of presenting a brief history of postcolonial theory within the length of a chapter I follow, more or less, Moore-Gilbert's formula. If nothing else, his division of the two camps along the rift of capital "T" theory affords the benefit of argumentative focus when contextualizing the last thirty years in the life of the discipline.

My overview of postcolonial theory is however far from being exhaustive, and it is such by design. I have opted for a selective reading over a summary one in order to accentuate a postcolonial politics of reading that involves reading as strategic rereading, forced reading, misreading, and reading as translation. This practice is one of catachresis. To cite Bhabha citing Spivak, catachresis as reading describes "the 'negotiation' of the postcolonial position 'in terms of reversing, displacing and seizing the apparatus of value-coding'" to constitute "a catachrestic space" out of the discourses of the West. This means wresting words and concepts from their meanings to rupture foreclosed moments, positions, and signifiers.[10] My attempt would be to rewrite both Western and non-Western postcolonial narratives by re-citing and re-siting these already contrived arenas for in-citing unhindered emergence of new and/or foreclosed-disavowed-repressed meanings.[11] My discussion of postcolonial theory is therefore purposefully selective, accented, and calibrated to pursue, promote, and perambulate *un*recognizable ideological positions in familiar texts to radically politicize our habits of reading.

The second chapter, "Postcolonial Theory and *Avatar*, Or, Postcolonial Criticism in a Multicultural World," comprises of postcolonial theoretical reading of a contemporary Hollywood film, namely James Cameron's immensely successful 2009 film *Avatar*. As this exercise is aimed at further supporting the arguments about the relevance of postcolonial theory in the era of globalization and at illustrating the veiled presence of Eurocentrism in contemporary discourses of the West, Cameron's film provides the perfect occasion for a postcolonial investigation. My analysis of the film will show, on the one hand, that Hollywood remains a most expedient vehicle for legitimizing Eurocentrism under the guise of liberalism and multiculturalism.

On the other hand, I wish to emphasize through my reading of the film that while the politics of othering the Other may indeed be no longer an issue in contemporary Western society and cultural texts, what is an issue for postcolonial analysis are the self-congratulatory critiques of the West's neocolonial ventures in the global South. James Cameron's *Avatar* repeats a rudimentary colonial imaginary drawn from the archives of imperial fantasy. Its formulaic narrative about a clash between a colonizing imperialist power and a self-respecting native culture is specifically set up to recall critically instances of European highhandedness against non-European Others in the past and the present. But underneath its rhetoric of multiculturalism, tolerant pluralism, ecological consciousness, and critique of the corporate militarism of the West, the film reproduces a narrative of European privilege and subject-production. *Avatar* is not about the Na'vi, the Other in the film. It thematizes our relation to the Other only to repossess otherness as what we already are or could be while excluding "*the real otherness of the Other*."[12]

Following Gayatri Chakravorty Spivak's cue about the excision of subaltern speech in discourses of the West (including self-critical and radical liberal discourses), I will argue for reading Cameron's film as one of the most current exegeses on reinventing the Western self. *Avatar* reminds me particularly of Spivak's reading of the character of the Magistrate in J.M. Coetzee's novel *Waiting for the Barbarians* (1980).[13] Spivak tells us that the Magistrate, whose logical composure is matched paradoxically by his inability to perform sexual acts with a young, attractive, captive barbarian woman, is trapped in the time of the Other, since he is seeking to know where he stands in the desire of this barbarian girl. The Magistrate's wish to know the Other's desire is an ineffective search for meaning around an irreducible otherness that cannot be integrated into any symbolic chain of signification. Care should be taken not to interpret the Magistrate's wish as a wanting to know the Other. The Magistrate is not interested to know anything about his captive except for what it means to be constituted in the desire of her automaton-like gaze. Spivak's assessment of the scene is invaluable. Otherness is constitutive of the magisterial self of Europe—the ungraspable, unfathomable other figures the self of Europe.[14]

Much in the same way, *Avatar* is not a film about the Na'vi, but, rather, about recuperating a self of Europe abstracted from current opinions of the West as neocolonial, habitually belligerent, and racially and culturally conservative. My reading argues, therefore, against routine understandings of the film as a critique of the West's long colonial history and its impact on indigenous populations and colonial ecologies. But I am equally opposed to hasty dismissals of the film as a clichéd racist narrative. For these foreclose any possibility of isolating the mechanisms through which a more insidious narrative of European privilege is enunciated. The film's real ideological aim is two-fold: first, to construct Sully as a rational knowledge-producing Western subject for the twenty-first century, and, second, to distract audiences from knowing anything about the real conditions afflicting the real indigenous populations of the world. My analysis consequently examines the narrative mechanics of Sully's subject formation and the filmic fantasy about an indigenous rebellion against the mercenaries of a tyrannical global military-corporation. *Avatar* is a disguised discourse of the West as the subject.

Notes

1 See Victor Li, "Globalization's Robinsonade: *Cast Away* and Neoliberal Subject Formation," in *Rerouting the Postcolonial: New Directions for the Millenium*, eds Janet Wilson, Cristina Sandru, and Sarah Lawson Welsh (New York: Routledge, 2010), 60–85.

2 Throughout this book "West" and "Europe" are used interchangeably. The words describe, to a lesser extent, the West European and transatlantic imperial powers such as England,

France, and the United States. To a greater extent, they denote a perspective located in the outlook of the Enlightenment that enables Europe to imagine itself as uniquely entitled to shape the history of the world.

3 I wonder at times, however, if rather than reimagining the future for postcolonial theory the crisis should occasion the opposite—time to stop investigating postcolonial's future.

4 Hamid Dabashi, "Can Non-Europeans Think? What Happens with Thinkers Who Operate Outside the European Philosophical 'Pedigree'?," *Al Jazeera* (January 15, 2013): www.aljazeera.com/indepth/opinion/2013/01/2013114142638797542.html.

5 See Gayatri Spivak, "Bonding in Difference: Interview with Alfred Artega (1993–94)," in *The Spivak Reader*, eds Donna Landry and Gerald Maclean (New York/London: Routledge, 1996), 28.

6 Robert Young, "Postcolonial Remains," *New Literary History* 43.1 (2012): 21, 22.

7 Robert Young has called Said, Bhabha, and Spivak the "holy-trinity" of postcolonial theory. Robert Young, *Colonial Desire: Hybridity in Theory, Culture, and Race* (London: Routledge, 1995), 154.

8 Bart Moore-Gilbert, *Postcolonial Theory: Contexts, Practices, Politics* (London/New York: Verso, 1997), 17.

9 Dennis Walder, *Post-colonial Literatures in English: History, Language, Theory* (Oxford: Blackwell, 1998), 72.

10 Homi Bhabha, "The Postcolonial and the Postmodern," *The Location of Culture* (London: Routledge, 1994), 263. For misreading as a postcolonial strategy for unraveling foreclosed meanings in imperial écriture, see also Gayatri Spivak, *A Critique of Postcolonial Reason: Towards a History of the Vanishing Present* (Cambridge: Harvard University Press, 1999).

11 Moore-Gilbert, *Postcolonial Theory*, 115.

12 Sergio Benvenuto, "Avatars of Otherness," *JEP-European Journal of Psychoanalysis* 28 (2009).

13 This example comes from Spivak's *Death of a Discipline* (New York: Columbia University Press, 2003). Spivak's entire book is extremely important in context of my work here. *Death of a*

Discipline is an exercise in reinventing comparative literature, apart from being an excellent counter to supposed postcolonial reservations about psychoanalytic theory. From the beginning to the end of her book, Spivak holds Freud close to the vision of a new comparative literature. She returns to psychoanalysis in order to defamiliarize her disciplinary home of comparative literature, to make it unhomely, only to reimagine a futurity out of that shocking rearrangement of disciplinary unhomeliness. In thinking and writing the "Introduction" I have also benefitted from reading Ian Almond's essay "Anti-Capitalist Objections to the Postcolonial: Some Conciliatory Remarks on Žižek and Context," *Ariel: a Review of Internatonal English Literature* 43.1 (2012): 1–21.

14 See Gayatri Chakravorty Spivak, "Can the Subaltern Speak?," in *Marxism and the Interpretation of Culture*, eds Cary Nelson and Lawrence Grossberg (Chicago: University of Chicago Press, 1988), 271–313.

CHAPTER ONE

The Postcolonial Avatar: A Brief History of Postcolonial Theory

The idea of the postcolonial

The idea of the postcolonial is inextricably tied to the establishment of colonies by European powers in diverse regions of Asia, the Americas, Africa, and Oceania. Though the word "colonialism" is etymologically derived from the Latin *colonia* meaning "farm" or "settlement," colonialism as discussed in this book does not refer to all historical instances of settling in another land. It refers specifically to modern or post-Enlightenment European colonizations. Radically different from all previous cases of colonization (including the Roman occupation of the British Isles around 50 CE and the establishment of Indianized kingdoms in Southeast Asia between the first and fourth centuries CE), modern colonialism refers to the forcible occupation of other lands, the control of these lands through various mechanisms of power, the resultant mutations of these colonial societies, and the legitimization of this occupation through the use of discourse. "Postcolonial" in this context is the disciplinary practice of studying the wide range of material and epistemic conditions emerging from colonial interactions between Europe and non-European societies during the colonial past, the decolonial interregnum, and the globalized neocolonial present.

Colonialism emerged in post-Enlightenment Europe in direct correlation with the growth of monopoly industrial capitalism and in conjunction with modernity. Stuart Hall terms colonialism the "outer face" of capitalist modernity. As colonial occupation of other lands enabled Europe to globalize the capitalist mode of production, a networked power relation was established "between and across nation-state frontiers and the *global/local* inter-relationships" drawing the colonies into complex and unequal social relationships of dependence with the West.[1] Produced through both coercion and ideological interpellation, these relations served to legitimize colonialism as not just an arbitrary exercise of power but as based on consent or lack of volition to give consent. Simply put, a characteristic feature of modern colonialism is its self-reflexive engagement with legitimizing its actions in the colony through discourses of natural law, divine sanction, and industrial enterprise. While the primary goal of colonialism remained the extraction of revenue through the exploitation of colonial resources and the labor of the colonized, the emphasis on subject formation and knowledge-production also remained palpably tied to the phenomenon of colonialism establishing recognizable planetary effects. Though direct forms of colonialism are absent today, Europe retains control over the globalized landscape through its control over and production of knowledge. "Subject making" occurs through the regulation of knowledge as colonialism and imperialism become neocolonialism and globalization.

Before moving forward, it is important to briefly distinguish imperialism and neocolonialism from colonialism. Though colonialism is often confused with imperialism and conflated with neocolonialism, both imperialism and neocolonialism are similar to yet different from colonialism. Imperialism is the repository of beliefs, interest, and discourses that ideologically underwrite the policies for administering the colonies.

The control of a colony in imperialism is not dependent on physical occupation of the land. Management of the colony is exercised indirectly through economic regulations of and the cultural recoding of the colonized society. Neocolonialism, on the other hand, is a displaced form of colonialism. It is displaced because its operative paradigms escape the habitual colonial and imperialist forms of structural exploitations of the non-Western Other. It retains the political dominance or hegemony of the West while appearing to promote shared prosperity and sustainable growth. In contrast to colonialism, neocolonialism disguises brutal exploitation under the rhetoric of social development and "just war," and, correspondingly, colonial institutions of coercion are replaced by a global credit economy.

The following historical and analytic categories constitute a foundation for thinking about the postcolonial:

(a) The time after colonialism (including the history of decolonial nation states as well as societies or communities that remain "colonized," exploited, marginalized within formerly colonized nations).

(b) The economic, social, and psychological legacies of colonialism (often identified as neocolonialism).

(c) The divergent experiences of colonialism and expressions of these experiences in cultural, political, and religious discourses by the colonized, formerly colonized, and colonizers during the colonial period and in the aftermath of decolonization (postcolonial literature, postcolonial film, etc.).

(d) The material, cultural, and affective rearrangements of the globe in the course of and in the aftermath of colonialism (arrangements that continue into our globalized present).

(e) The ideological positions adopted during anti-colonial and anti-imperial resistances to colonialism and imperialism (nationalist/revolutionary wars of colonial liberation), and ideological positions assumed today in opposition to globalization and neocolonialism.

What is postcolonial theory?

It has become almost customary to begin a book on postcolonial theory with an observation about the difficulty of defining the term "postcolonial" and thereafter reflecting on the multiple ways in which the term has been defined, debated, and misread over the years. The postcolonial is a notoriously difficult term to define. Yes, but this is not because of any inherent contradiction within the discipline or the multiple conceptions of the discipline or even due to misreadings of it. Nor is it a sign of intellectual dynamism. Rather, the reason why many postcolonial theorists recuse themselves from offering singular, watertight definitions to questions such as "What is postcoloniality?" or "What is postcolonial theory?" has to do with the politics of the postcolonial itself.

Postcolonial theorists are distrustful of ontological questions, grand narratives, and universal definitions. It is a political and philosophical countermanding of the need for a transcendental signifier universally establishing meaning across societies, cultures, and history. It is a rejection of the Enlightenment vision of the West as the universal in complete dismissal of particular histories, provincial truths, and pluralized cultures. Postcolonial theory is the methodology for critically examining the varied histories, experiences, and expressions of colonialism as it affected peoples, cultures, societies, ecologies, and nonhumans across the globe (and continues to affect, one may add). The theory does not provide all the answers but rather a basis that enables critical examinations of complex and often speciously intertwined practices of European colonialism and its lingering legacies. Postcolonial theory does not provide a coherent set of beliefs but instead a starting point for inquiry into beliefs.

An important area of postcolonial theoretical focus has been narratives of European self-determination and the placement of the non-European Other within these narratives. Postcolonial theory tirelessly interrogates the processes through which Europe occupied, controlled, and "reformed" colonized societies (both physically and discursively); Europe's strategic managerial interventions into colonial economy, military, and culture; its overall use of discourse to justify colonial occupation through "self-evident" universal truths (scientific as well as religious); and the colonized's diverse negotiations of imperial hegemony and postcoloniality (sometimes through resistance, at other times through sly civility and mimicry). Put another way, postcolonial theory investigates processes through which Europe constitutes its position as a sovereign locus of truth and power via appropriation of and control over the modes of knowledge-production. It is the West's control over mechanisms of knowledge-production that gives it the power to write itself into histories of entitlement. Postcolonial theory probes this unwarranted anointment of Europe and its affective impact on human lives globally.

It is common for postcolonial theory to consider the West's writing of history through examinations of its rhetorical distancing of itself from and its symbolic repossessing of the Other in discourse. This manner of investigation, while leading toward identification of the native Other as a recalcitrant stain on the West's historical imagination, remains caught up within the West's prejudiced representational regime. The critical practice of recuperating marginalized voices constitutes one of the more popular directions of postcolonial theoretical analysis. Yet it does not represent the full range and potential of postcolonial theory. Its limits are constantly evident and inevitably produce disappointment with the ineffectiveness of this political strategy. Just to be clear, we should not dismiss entirely the value of retrieving and mainstreaming the marginal Other, but at the same time we can not be content with arguments that suggest such acts of rehabilitation of the colonized Other are either the only or should be the most important task of postcolonial theory. A rejection of the dominant universal in favor of the diminutive particular does not imply that the task of postcolonial theory is only to reintegrate the particular into the universal, which is what retrieving the marginalized Other does.

Similarly, questions such as "Why is the Other represented derogatorily?" and "What facilitated this disparaging representation?," while critical for understanding the colonizer/colonized or oppressor/oppressed binary, fail often to broaden sufficiently into determining the role played by the Other's unsymbolizable radical otherness in discourses of the West. Compared to practices aimed at representing excised voices and those interrogating the processes of that excision, a crucial task of postcolonial theory remains representing the excised marginal as an interruption in the dominant regime. The enigmatic otherness of the Other always escapes acts of imperial nomination designating the teeming multitude of the colony as singular. This fleeting otherness disrupts the imperial perspective and compels imperial discourse to repeat its dramatizations of authority over the colonized, thereby exposing the unbridgeable gap constitutive of the West's subjective ontology. If postcolonial theorists like Edward Said, Homi Bhabha, and Gayatri Spivak teach us anything it is this: the native Other constitutes an enigma that cannot be incorporated into the West's symbolic order of meaning without the otherness being made contingent on the self of Europe. Postcolonial theorists in the twenty-first century would be better off embracing this unincorporated otherness rather than staying satisfied with the limited practice of studying the mechanisms of prejudiced representations of the Other.

Postcolonial theory is an interruption in the Anglo-American university discourse. It follows the rules of academic and institutional engagement, and yet it stays willfully negligent of the established protocols of Enlightenment reading and interpretation. If it analyzes dominant cultural discourses for unraveling manifest and latent signatures of Eurocentrism, then it equally challenges the work done under the auspices of the Anglo-American university, including work done under the rubric of postcolonial studies, for being complicit in the cultural production of meaning that ultimately privileges the West.

Postcolonial theory is geared toward bringing into light the lacunas in the West's narratives of genesis. Postcolonial theory is not just hermeneutics or a way of reading. It takes on a more active position as it unravels the role of the debased and the noble Other in European narratives to constitutively change the character of these narrations. Postcolonial theory and theorizations of the postcolonial work under erasure to underscore the irreducible heterogeneity of the Other against the assumed singularity that European discourse assigns to this Other. In other words, postcolonial theory capsizes characteristic narratives of immaculate beginnings, peripatetic crises, and synthesized teleological ends. Postcoloniality is a challenge to the unconditional desire for meaning as a guarantee of the genuine being of the empire against the nothingness of the colony.

Postcolonial theory today

Postcolonial theory stands at a critical juncture today. At stake is the question of its relevance in the age of globalization. More pertinently, the question that the contemporary situation poses is whether postcolonial theory is adequate for examining the manifold complexities of global capitalism. Some believe it is time to move on, leaving postcolonial theory behind. Others urge for situating it in dialogue with modalities of thinking that are better suited to the global present. And a handful, including Robert Young, remain convinced of the usefulness of postcolonial theory for inquiring into the politics of invisibility, unreadability, and revisionism that continue to underwrite the structures of European oppression over the rest of the globe. Irrespective of these debates the general opinion is that the postcolonial is dead and we are already in a post-postcolonial moment.

Critiques of postcolonial theory in recent years have come from three rather unequal partners: the Indian-American sociologist Vivek Chibber; the Indian-American entrepreneur-turned-Hinduvta-apologist, Rajiv Malhotra; and the Slovenian philosopher Slavoj Žižek. Though Chibber and Malhotra have called postcolonial theory's continued relevance into question, they have done so in inconsistent and often unsubstantial ways that others, including Gayatri Spivak, have already dissected and exposed. Chibber and Malhotra are nonetheless representative of a certain line of critique and thus merit a brief mention. Žižek's few assertions about postcolonial theory, however, require a bit more attention because they capture the general orientation of much of routine criticism about the discipline raised over approximately the last thirty years.

Žižek summarizes the ailing state of postcolonial studies in passing in his 2002 essay "A Plea for Leninist Intolerance." While agreeing that the postcolonial question is crucial, he deplores the trend in postcolonial studies to translate issues of economic and class inequality into a "multiculturalist problematic of the colonized minorities' right to narrate their victimizing experience."[2] The enfolding of the postcolonial problematic in the multiculturalist ideology implies only one thing for Žižek—a revisioning of colonial conflict as the Other's right to speak her side of the story. Can the Other's right to produce a counternarrative dismantle the axiomatic habits of listening that block out the Other's voice? Žižek rightly asks. In other words, Žižek says that the politics of colonialism cannot be resolved by reintegrating and representing the excised Other as a valid voice. This gesture might attest to our tolerance toward the Other as a foreign outside or as the foreigner inside ourselves, but it does not address the economic struggle integral to the colonial conflict. As a result, the political and economic conflict becomes, for Žižek, an internal conflict playing out within the Western psyche and thereby denuded of its political and economic core. And who is responsible for this? According to Žižek, the Third World intellectual working as a postcolonial theorist in the First World academy.

While some scholars have associated Žižek's attitude toward postcolonialism with his overt Eurocentrism, the more important point to be made here is that Žižek's criticisms are neither new nor idiosyncratic.[3] This is one reason why we should take them seriously. Žižek's two primary points—first, postcolonial theory has distanced itself from the political–economic struggles of the Third World replacing these with cultural studies style textual analysis, and, second, that Third World scholars in the Anglo-American academy pursue puerile *games of identity politics* under the pretext of "doing" postcolonial studies—have been made before by postcolonial critics such as Aijaz Ahmad, Benita Parry, Arif Dirlik, Abdul JanMohamed, and Ella Shohat. Like Žižek, these scholars, too, have accused postcolonial theory of depoliticizing colonial history and alleged its complicity with neocolonialism by noting the postcolonial privileging of cultural analyses over political readings of the (post)colony.

Aijaz Ahmad, for instance, anticipates Žižek's contentions by at least a decade in *In Theory* (1992). Here, Ahmad criticizes the affective hold of theorists like Foucault, Derrida, and Lacan on postcolonial theory and judges the latter "methodologically and empirically" faulty because of this hold.[4] As proof, he notes postcolonial theory's disengagement of focus from Third World socio-economic struggles and its privileging of textual analysis. With the political Third World reconstituted as the cultural world of the postcolonial by means of a privileging of the moment of European colonialism, postcolonial theory limits the narratives from these Other lands to responses to the experience of colonialism. Thus emptied of their heterogeneous histories, the postcolonial worlds appear as nothing but theoretical categories that reduce them to a singular structure. Ahmad therefore advises postcolonial theorists working in the West to question their own subjective constitution by the First World conditions of knowledge-production. In essence, Ahmad accuses postcolonial theorists of packaging Third World literature, history, and culture into bite-sized consumable products for the consumption of the West.[5]

Similar reservations run through the writings of Abdul JanMohamed and Arif Dirlik.[6] JanMohamed claims for instance in his important 1985 essay "The Economy of Manichean Allegory" that the colonizer–colonized relationship is essentially dichotomous and profoundly antagonistic. He urges accordingly that postcolonial theory focus on the economic and historical contexts within the colonial situation. This would enable us to see how the opposition against colonialism actually articulated itself. Arif Dirlik's *The Postcolonial Aura* raises the same allegation against postcolonial theory's tendency to refract material realities through problems of braided subjectivity and theories of infinite deferral of signification. Dirlik blames French theory and postmodernism for corrupting the political agency of anti-colonial perspectives and upbraids the Third World critic teaching in the First World universities for facilitating such intellectual irregularities.

The most persistent and the most trenchant critiques of postcolonial theory have come from Benita Parry.[7] For Parry, the linguistic turn of the 1970s in the academy is responsible for leading postcolonial theory astray. She charges postcolonial theorists for being willfully negligent about anti-colonial resistance and substituting discursive cultural configurations for material contexts. In *Postcolonial Studies*, she chastises postcolonial theory for being myopic and accuses postcolonial theorists for unnecessarily problematizing colonialism. She says that under the influence of "post" theories, postcolonial theory has abandoned historical and social explanations of capital revising the site of the colony into a network of signs and signifiers. In this way, it effects an elision of the material world.

Parry is most disappointed with Homi Bhabha and Gayatri Spivak. Their theorizations of the colony and postcolony, she argues, are responsible for silencing native voices and for replacing colonizer–colonized oppositional politics with discussions about epistemic violence and discursive subjectivity. Parry urges instead for a return to the fundamental condition of colonialism as identified in the writings of Frantz Fanon. That is, colonialism as a life and death struggle between two irreconcilable forces. To her it is imperative that the colonized speak, that the colonized actively participate in writing an alternative that responds to colonialism and looks toward a different future.

While Parry correctly insists on the identification of colonialism with conflictual politics, she is too sanguine about the ability of the colonized to articulate their own history. Given the material and epistemic entanglement of the colony under colonialism, it is not possible to write back without submitting to the axiomatic structures of Western episteme. It is not possible to historicize colonized identity outside the context of the cultural and political dominance of the West. The influence of Europe on all history makes it impossible to write postcolonial history by simply wishing Europe and its dominance away. In this context, it is an open question whether the colonized or formerly colonized can really write a new history. For example, one cannot simply revalidate the cyclical histories of South Asia or rehabilitate Igbo understanding of "aesthetic value as *process* rather than *product*" without falling into the traps of ethno-nationalism and revivalism.[8] What is more, the native's desire to be part of, to participate in, and to lay claim to history, is essentially a desire structured by its Other, the West. The invitation to participate in history, to politicize native destinies, comes first from the West as a conditional invitation.

Native desire to write history is a desire to wield the power of signification over the precolonial past—to reclaim, reconstitute, and reimagine the past in order to posit it against the colonial present and in continuity with the decolonial future. As such, this history is ideologically presented as a counter-narrative to colonial historiography, though in most cases it is rhetorically imagined in relation to European history. In colonial Bengal, for example, Bankim Chandra Chatterjee famously complained about the native's lack of history as a serious handicap to the formation of the Bengali cultural identity. In "Banglar Itihas" (The History of Bengal) and "Banglar Itihas Sombondhe Koyekti Katha" (Few Words Relative to the History of Bengal), he writes, "If the Europeans go out bird hunting, a history of it is written. But Bengal does not have a history. Greenland has its written history, even the Maoris have some sort of history, but the land that has witnessed civilizations like

Gaur, cities like Tamralipta and Saptagram . . . that country has no history . . . Bengal needs its history, else the Bengali can never achieve greatness."[9] What is folded into Bankim's ethno-nationalist desire to retrieve the glorious lost history of Bengal is the ideological need for the colonized to assume control over vernacular knowledge-production. Writing history is not a documentary or empirical project; it is an ideological project aimed at regaining the means of subject-making. But unfortunately, the past that the native hopes to retrieve in order to realign his nationalist history does not exist. It exists insofar as colonialism has narrated it.

Colonialism has been historically responsible for imagining lost native pasts to ordain its historical legitimacy to rule the colony. The tripartite periodization of South Asian history that James Mill conceives in his 1817 book *The History of British India* followed the Whig-Utilitarian conception of history as linear and progressive to divide subcontinental history into three distinct phases—the Hindu past, the Muslim interregnum, and the Christian present. Implicit in this division was the suggestion that the Muslim period in Indian history rendered void the glories of the Hindu past so that the Christian present could be explained as a period of reawakening for the Indian masses. Colonialism guides the Indians back on the path of progress. It is a gross injustice to read Mill's *History* in isolation, however. Other orientalists such as William Jones and Max Muller contributed to the image of a golden Hindu past and to the Romantic idealization of the colonized subject as a noble savage living in the desirable wholeness of Nature. Though the orientalist valorization of a non-European Sanskrit past seems to run counter to a vision that sees Europe as the pinnacle of history, the two actually fit together well. Both share a quasi-Hegelian rationale that sees the spirit of history residing in India before moving to Europe. Furthermore, the idea of wholeness discovered in the Indian past appeals to the Romantic consciousness of the time. The colonial discourse contrasts the appetitive Muslim interval to the spirited but lost Hindu past, a contrast that justifies the rational British present.

This same fantastic discourse fed the nineteenth-century Indian nationalist imaginaries and is responsible for the Hindu-Indian identity that is being promoted by the Hindu Right in India today. The ideological effects of colonialism are pervasive and deep and inescapable.

In the face of demands that the colonized historicize their destiny, postcolonial theory envisions an alternate response. Rather than adding the colonized voice to the chorus of history, one can opt out of the game of historical recognition. One need not be recognized as a historical subject in order to have a politicized subjectivity. One can reject the European primacy of history and refuse to participate in history. In order to imagine how this might look, we can consider the last scene in Gillo Pontecorvo's *Queimada/Burn!* (1969). At the crack of dawn on the morning of José Dolores's (Evaristo Marquez) execution, agent William Walker (Marlon Brando) meets the revolutionary. Walker is there to set him free. He knows a dead, martyred revolutionary is more dangerous than a live, discredited one, and he is certain that Dolores will gladly accept an offer of freedom rather than dying on the gallows. But Dolores refuses to escape. He prefers death to the white man's offer of freedom and says to Walker, "If a man gives you freedom, it is not freedom. Freedom is something you, you alone must take." One can read in Dolores's refusal a dismissal of European civilization and its economy of desires. For as he tells Walker, who is perplexed by Dolores's reluctance to escape, "If what we have in our country is civilization, civilization of White Man [that is, Europe], then we are better uncivilized, because it is better to know where to go and not know how, than it is to know how to go and not know where." In this scene Dolores teaches us a very important lesson: it is impossible to escape the pervasive hold of colonialism without fully alienating one's colonized self from the economy of imperial desire.

The colonized must become thoroughly uprooted before the imperial assemblage can be dismantled. In choosing death over life, Dolores makes an ethical decision. We should not read death in this scene as just the end of the physical body, but also as a performance of radical alienation from colonized subjectivity. Just as he cannot continue to enjoy English whisky and be an anti-colonial revolutionary at the same time, similarly he cannot accept the lease of life from an Englishman and live truly free. Accepting Walker's offer to escape and live free would cause Dolores to live in Walker's debt for the rest of his life. And this is unacceptable to Dolores because his entire struggle was against the debt imposed on his land and his people by the West and their comprador agents. As he says, "If they let me live, it means it is convenient for them. And if it is convenient for them, it is convenient for me to die." Through death Dolores thus fully abstracts himself from the colonizer–colonized dialectic otherwise impossible to achieve within colonialism. A life of debt is not a life at all. Hence, if Dolores is to hold onto his desire to live free—that is, to live without being in economic, political, and cultural debt of the West—he has to stand up against Europe's interest in the Antilles. He must constantly struggle against the social order arranged by and for the preservation of European interests in his island nation. Agent Walker rightly suspects in the film that death will only make Dolores invincible. He will cease to be just a person and will become an idea that Europe cannot control. Through the freedom articulated by his death, Dolores limits imperialism's structure of and desire for complete control. His disembodied presence in inspirational songs renders him outside of colonial hegemony and enables him to disrupt it.

The figure of Dolores stands in contrast to the figure of another anti-colonial revolutionary in cinema, the nationalist revolutionary Sandip, in Satyajit Ray's 1984 adaptation of Rabindranath Tagore's *Ghare-Baire* (*The Home and the World*). Sandip (Soumitra Chatterjee), a firebrand *swadeshi* (nationalist) leader advocating complete boycott of all things British has only one weakness: imported British cigarettes. He has sacrificed everything tainted by association with Britain—clothes, his job, even the English language—but he detests the local or *deshi* cigarettes. It is precisely this inability to sever all connections with the English that leads to the gradual unfolding of Sandip as a hypocrite and charlatan. The contrast between his public call for nationalism or *swadeshi* and his private indulgence in British cigarettes leads to his downfall in the film. The point made in both films is the need for total and unconditional liberation from the visible as well as invisible structures of imperial rule. Liberation from a colonial regime can never be conditional, negotiated, or bartered. It is not a discovery of self rather an alienation from the self. Rewriting of national history in order to claim it against colonial historiography is as counter-productive to decolonization as is the argument for the formerly colonized finding representation in history.

The issue with postcolonial theory today is not that it is incapable of interrogating the changed conditions of the global planet. To the contrary, it continues to remain a useful tool for investigating Europe's manipulation of knowledge-production for the purposes of subject formation. However, in order to acutely examine the fine texture of twenty-first-century global politics, postcolonial theory must first alienate itself from the institutional status it enjoys. Postcolonial theory can buttress a symbolic identity but must serve as a force that constantly undermines any such identity. This is the only way that it can avoid becoming part of the imperial regime that it aims to contest. The failures of postcolonial theory in the globalized world have not been the result of excessive theorizing and too little attention to history but rather the abandonment of the theorizing that would enable it to remain vigilant about its own institutionalization. *The real problem with postcolonial theory is not that it is too theoretical but that it is not theoretical enough.*

The man who drank his own pee

The current state of institutional postcolonial theory reminds me of a story my *thakuma* (Bengali for paternal grandmother) once shared with me. It is the story of the *man who drank his pee* and it is as follows:

> A man from Sylhet was on a journey to the City. He was carrying with him parched rice for the trip; but he forgot to carry water. In the middle of his long march he stopped by a river to get water for soaking the parched rice. But every time he neared the water, a big fish would float up and scare him away. After several tries the harried man shooed the fish from the safety of the bank and said: *ami muitya chira bhijamu kintu jole namum na*! (I'll pee and soak my parched rice in it but I will not dip into your water.)

The Sylheti man's refusal to persevere pointedly resonates with the general hesitancy on the part of some postcolonial theorists to reimagine the discipline by taking the necessary if risky step into theory. This has, for the most part, resulted in postcolonial theory remaining smugly complacent with interrogating discursive constructions of subjectivity and textual politics.

The role of neoliberal individualism and capitalist economics in the constitution of the academy may indeed be one reason for the failure of postcolonial theory to critically examine the global present. But at the same time, a general distrust of theory or "doing theory" is equally responsible for further stultifying the ability to extend postcolonial theoretical analyses of globalization toward what Gayatri Spivak terms "*productive crises*." This caution has only ended up promoting an adamantine practice of "information-retrieval" performed with "self-conscious rectitude" following "a deliberately 'nontheoretical' methodology."[10] Like the Sylheti man soaking his sustenance in his own urine, thus not wasting any bodily fluid and recirculating the abject back inside the bounds of his body, postcolonial theory too has been reduced in the wake of a moribund reticence toward "doing theory" to producing and consuming self-same analyses of the West's prejudiced representations of the East.

There is nothing inherently wrong with this direction of analysis, but it suits the dispensations of a neocolonial West and its university discourse very well. For the politics of excavating Others lost due to the past of European colonialism complements

Europe's current guilt-induced critical assessments of its own histories. The rehabilitation of lost Others in mainstream discourse also gels well with Europe's current disposition toward tolerant pluralism and multiculturalism. And in the context of the increasing number of terrorist attacks throughout Europe, it helps the West to present its liberal subjectivity by saying "we tried to bring them closer to us, make them part of our social life, but they still hate us!" These new modes of repossessing the Other—these new modes of colonialism—can be challenged only by resuscitating the real otherness of the Other. Postcolonial theory in the present needs to expand its identification and critique of European systems of signification as violent apparatuses of domination. It needs to take the complementary step following on from this to identifying the Other as irreducible to and defiant of European systems of signification, and as such symptomatic of a split within the identity of Europe itself.

Those who believe that postcolonial theory is more than an academic discipline, that it is an activism against the West's perpetration of systemic injustices throughout the world, should readily admit that criticisms of prejudiced representations of the Other and recuperations of excised voices do nothing to change the West's view of the Other. It is useful to recall here Edward Said's poignant reminder early on in *Orientalism* that "one ought never to assume that the structure of Orientalism is nothing more than a structure of lies and myths which, were the truth about them be told, would simply blow away."[11] In fact, by limiting the function of postcolonial theory to exploring representation, we are further enabling the West to appropriate our voices, voices that, according to some, have already been domesticated by the universities in the West. The point is not that all postcolonial theorists in the First World academy should resign immediately; instead, they must engage in a profound articulation of genuine love. The postcolonial theorist in the First World academy has to alienate herself radically from her subjectivity and alienate her discipline from itself.

Postcolonial theory needs to be more and not less theoretically rigorous. We need to openly advocate for the radicalization of postcolonial theory, that is, the retheorization of the postcolonial critical imaginary. And, if one of the ways to do this requires bringing postcolonial theory closer to high theory, so be it. I disagree that French theory or any other Western theory is responsible for misleading postcolonial theory. The problem, as I see it, is not that postcolonial theory mediated by Foucault, Derrida, or Lacan is incapable of undertaking an intellectually thorough analysis of colonial or neocolonial politics, but rather that the use of such theories in the context of colonialism and postcoloniality have never been rigorous enough. As such, the correct response to criticisms of postcolonial theory's interfaces with French theory should entail a paradoxical call to return to the writings of Foucault, Derrida, and Lacan with greater intellectual conviction. We cannot, however, do this by constantly apologizing for the unfortunate theoretical exercises that may have come before. We cannot be apprehensive like the Sylheti man about entering the murky "waters" of high theory because of its Eurocentric undercurrent; instead, we should be confident that once exposed to postcolonial theory's persistent critique a distilled critical vision would remain to use in postcolonial analysis. We also cannot stage a conditional return by leaving out some theories while working with others. To put it bluntly: we cannot reimagine postcolonial theory by apologizing first for such bugbears as Homi Bhabha and his use of Lacanian psychoanalysis and Derridean deconstruction. The question whether Bhabha's use of theory was appropriate or not is moot here. More important is the necessity of returning to postcolonial theory the valuable lenses of Derrida and Lacan.[12]

Postcolonial theory is a theory constantly in the process of formation. Infused with the Socratic imperative for self-examination, the discipline operates under the mark of erasure—it auto-critiques itself, remains inconclusive, and is articulated only as difference. Postcolonial auto-critique is an exercise in self-evaluation pursued through a constant critique of the desire to conceptualize postcolonialism as a structured system with one true moment of origin and a distinguishable end. It is an attempt to modify the inside of the discipline alongside transgressing the said discipline but without appearing as a *fait accompli*. As such the lot of the postcolonial theorist is to critique the structure she calls her disciplinary home.

The holy trinity *plus* one

A review of the writings of Said, Bhabha, and Spivak is the starting point for reimagining postcolonial theory in the present. Alongside these three I will also consider a fourth thinker, namely Frantz Fanon. My reasons for including Fanon are categorical. First, he has a profound influence on the "holy trinity"; second, he is one of the most theoretically oriented anti-colonial thinkers from the mid-twentieth century; third, postcolonial critics like Parry have been asking for a return to Fanon for retooling postcolonial theory; and, fourth, as I discuss later in this chapter, Fanon's theories were instrumental in inspiring the Third Cinema movement in the 1960s and continues to remain useful for postcolonial analysis of cinema.

Frantz Fanon

Black Skin, White Masks (1952), *A Dying Colonialism* (1959), *The Wretched of the Earth* (1961), and the posthumously published *Toward the African Revolution* (1964) constitute the primary mass of Frantz Fanon's (1925–1961) anti-colonial writing. Fanon's premature death from leukemia in 1961 cut short his intellectual output, but it did not limit his influence. Partly based on his own personal experiences of racial prejudice in Paris and partly based on his professional work as a psychiatrist treating both white and black patients, *Black Skin, White Masks* is an analysis of subject formation within a hostile, racially divided, and classed world. Together with *The*

Wretched of the Earth, it aims to recover and rebuild lost Black culture by means of self-awakening achieved through revolutionary violence against all forms of colonial domination.

Rebutting institutional and popular explanations of racial stereotypes, such as Octave Mannoni's theory of "dependency complex," Fanon argues for recognizing racism as an epiphenomenon of colonialism. In particular, he stresses that the imposition of the colonizer's language on the colonized is responsible for redacting all pre-existing cultural identities and forcing the black man to wear a white mask. Forced into this role-playing, the colonized becomes suspended in the time and desire of the West. On the one hand, the colonized subject attempts to live up to the expectations of the West that she or he always fails to meet. On the other hand, the colonized subject has to linger in a phantasmagorical liminal space between the mask and her or his skin.[13] To a black subject wearing a white mask, the promised utopia of *assimilation* always remains distant. The Frenchified black man in Paris, as Fanon's anecdotes painfully capture, remains captive of a "racial epidermal schema"—a monster "battered down by tom-toms, cannibalism, intellectual deficiency, fetishism, racial defects, slave-ships" and deformity—yet charged with performing the routine of European modernity even in the face of omnipresent racial insults.[14] The consequent disjunction between body and mind, Fanon contends, creates the native as a deracinated and alienated subject. Crime in the community and mental illness are direct results of this dispossession, and these social problems express an unconscious drive toward mending the distortion of the body and mind.

Fanon's great achievement consists in his politicization of colonial culture, society, and identity. While Western institutional knowledge sought to explain crime in the colony as resulting from cultural traits of the colonized, Fanon puts the horse before the cart by holding colonial occupation, dislocation and exploitation of the natives as responsible for social crimes. At the same time, he transcends the trap of reactionary identity politics by pointing out how colonialism equally affects the colonizer. The black and white binary that emerges in the wake of imperialism constitutes each subject's identity by way of a Hegelian dialectic wherein the white colonizer needs the existence-in-negation of the black colonized to constitute his or her own identity as the colonizer. In this dialectic, while the "black man wants to be white [the] white man slaves to reach a human level."[15] This valuable observation regarding the white man's servitude often gets lost in reading Fanon. But it is crucial to bring this point to the center of a discussion on Fanon since it establishes the colonizer–colonized relationship as more than a recalibration of the Hegelian master–slave dialectic. If we consider the argument that the black dehumanized subject lends the white its "human" lease, we can view colonial discourse through the lens of biopolitics: colonial discourse marks the black dehumanized subject as bare life, as life that is not properly human. The colonized Other acquires its identity through a primordial negation that renders this bare life open to the most ruthless acts of exploitation of colonized bodies and labor. And in this way, colonial discourse folds a certain nonhuman traumatic otherness into the creation of the Other. Rather than excising otherness, this discourse includes "it" as incipient in the image of the Other.

In *The Wretched of the Earth*, Fanon continues his psychoanalytic analysis of colonialism couched in a radical rhetoric for organized political action, including militant resistance against all forms of colonial domination. Describing the colonial universe as a Manichean world, Fanon advocates absolute violence against imperial domination—a total war of national liberation led by the peasants against the structures of colonial hegemony. Fanonian violence aims at liberation through dismantling of existing structures of governance; complete deconstruction and reconstitution of the nation state; and, the forging of a new consciousness and a New Man. As Fanon explains, "the 'thing' colonized becomes a man through the very process of liberation."[16] Revolutionary violence aims at much more than national independence from foreign rule; it calls for a purging and decoupling of the colonized from the oppressive colonial socio-psychological machinery. Total liberation involves cleansing of all images that the colonial systems produce and the subsequent evolution of a national consciousness free from the sphere of bourgeois values and crony capitalism that infect the colony. It is, above all, the recommencement of a new history that is necessarily located at the end of the struggle. If it fails, the post-independence decolonized state would become nothing but a caricature of the colonizing state. Even worse, it risks turning virtual from inner contradictions and collapsing eventually. Absolute violence is necessary to prevent this from occurring. Fanon's absolute violence is an ethical act that seeks to achieve a moment of radical subjective destitution, that is, the moment when the subject recognizes the true face of the colonial system as arbitrary and dehumanized. It is the crucial moment of resistance since the subject exposes the truth and refuses to act within it.

Homi Bhabha rightly infers that reading Fanon today one enters a crepuscular world where revolutionary idealism morphs into post-9/11 anxiety over terrorism.[17] But we should not forget that a vicious hegemonic stranglehold that justifies its actions through the transcendent authority of capital can only be dismantled by an equal, oppositional violence. What we are witnessing today—Islamofascism locked in an unending war with the liberal democratic West leading to the creation of a perpetual state of emergency that justifies the suspension of the law—is merely the inverse of what the nineteenth century witnessed in the name of colonialism. Then, the West on the pretext of serving the divine duty to civilize the dark recesses of the world was locked in opposition with the colonies. Today, the Islamofascists are claiming that it is their divine duty to educate the uninitiated West onto the one true path of enlightenment. These moments are not historically disjointed; rather, what is truly unfolding today is the continuation of and the effect of Europe's colonial exertions of power, and this is reason number one why Fanon retains his relevance.

Edward Said

Published in 1978, Edward Said's *Orientalism* is commonly identified as the starting point of postcolonial theory in the academy. *Orientalism* is a groundbreaking study of the West's habitual representations of the East, or non-West, through a limited, negative repository of images—the non-European as savage, lazy, barbarous, lascivious, despotic, timeless, full of unimaginable riches untapped by the docile inhabitants, etc. These and other similar figurations of the East by the West, Said contends, constitute a representational praxis that functions to append the East as an Other to the Self of Europe.[18] The production of the East—that is, the stereotyping of the East—is the production of knowledge about the East. The discursive imaginings of the non-West as a homogenous Other through epistemology (philosophy, science) and representational praxis (art, literature) serve to consolidate European hegemony over non-European societies. The way knowledge about the East is acquired and produced is not, however, objective, natural, self-evident, and universal, as the West typically claims. Rather the initial production of this knowledge and its reproduction in Western cultural discourses function tendentiously to secure the privilege of Europe over the non-West.

Said's thesis concerning the relation between knowledge, power, and hegemony is simple yet tidy. Drawing from Michel Foucault, Said states that the objective behind knowing the Orient was to control it. Knowledge operates as a form of power. This theory finds immediate corroboration in the South Asian context where, to an extent, the colonial regime was dependent upon establishing, preserving, and interpreting local customs (a completely fortuitous method of engaging with the Other by constructing otherness at the level of broad imaginary signifiers of difference) with knowledge functioning as an institutional system of support. In many of his subsequent works, Said continued to demonstrate the relation between imperial praxis and cultural productions while detailing analytic methods for uncovering these. *Covering Islam: How the Media and the Experts Determine How We See the Rest of the World* (1981) describes its project in the subtitle; *The World, the Text, the Critic* (1983) emphasizes the worldliness of texts or the need to read texts by situating them in history; and *Culture and Imperialism* (1993) accentuates the complicity of European canonized, cultural texts in conserving the hegemony of the West, while advocating what Said calls a contrapuntal reading as a strategy for excavating local histories buried under, intertwined with, and transformed by the behemoth of Western history.

Orientalism offers a methodology for identifying and probing the hidden relationship between Western constructions of knowledge and Western exercises of power. But the book also leads us toward discerning a close association between Western cultural representation and the subject-production of the West. Subjectivity of the West is convened in cultural texts through both mis-representation and missed representations of the Other. Both forms of representation are arranged through visible and invisible gestures of foreclosure, disavowal, and repression of the non-Western other in order to constitute the Other's identity-in-difference from the self of Europe. It is crucial that a distinction is made between the Other, representing the symbolic identity of the native constituted as different from the identity of the West, and the other which represents all that is enigmatic, radical, and unsymbolizable in the non-West. The other is the heterogeneous, risky, vernacular dispensation of the Other that remains unrecuperable in and defiant of the West's cognitive-nominative maps. The Other is an attempt to domesticate this otherness. Put differently, otherness endangers circuits of imperial production and ruptures colonial discipline. The Other in colonial discourse functions to overwrite this enigmatic otherness thereby reproducing the colony as congenitally riven by an absence-in-presence.

Postcolonial theory following Said must investigate the relation of this other to colonial representation. It needs to ask what do repeated fictional and non-fictional discursive returns to this other indicate about the West's ontological being and its sadomasochistic desire for experiencing the discomfort of a mute, unknown other. This compulsion to encounter the unpleasurable might demonstrate the West's drive toward its own destruction and death, and it might also show how the West requires an image of the other as death in order to constitute itself. With this way of thinking about the West in relation to otherness, postcolonial theory can approach the issue of misrepresentation in colonial discourse with the requisite complexity.

We can examine a common image of colonial discourse—the unnamed Arab on the television screen. The documentary entitled *On Orientalism*, based on the book and featuring Said, begins by showing a series of orientalized images from Hollywood films interspersed with television footage of Arabs and the oriental paintings of Eugène Delacroix and Jean-Léon Gérome. This mix of images shows a communication between the real representations and fictional depictions of the "Arab." In each case, these images stereotype the Arab as excessively belligerent against the West and prepared to do it harm. At first, one simply wants to denounce these images as racist stereotypes. But this prevents us from seeing why the stereotypes arise and the drive that produces the images. The images of fierce Arabs that we see regularly on television—chanting for the death of the United States—are not simply racist misrepresentation but acts of ethical representation by the West. These images showcase the West's structural inability to "see" the Other in any way except as the harbinger of death. The other whose incomprehensible speech renders her unknown except as an unreadable signature of the Other indexes a lack in the Western cognition and its ability to control the Other through knowledge. The unbearable other is thus a threat and the only way to negotiate its presence is by rendering it absent.

Misrepresentation obviously assumes that there is a proper representation that is possible. In other words, unlike the

"Arabs" we see on television there are other kinds of Arabs whom we do not get to see on screen. The understanding seems to be that if these Arabs are brought into the limelight, Western prejudice against and misrepresentation of Arabs would cease. Interestingly, this belief finds an ideological parallel in the commonplace question often asked in the post-9/11 world, "Why do they hate us?" But questions such as this (and the corollary, "Are there Arabs who do not hate us?") never really seek an answer. No one asks these questions with the belief that an answer from the Other explaining her stance against the West could put an end to the global conflict. The multicultural West shows an interest in the Other but does not want to hear what otherness has to say. This inability to hear the Other helps to justify the exercise of power over the Other. Similarly, the search for a peaceful, tolerant, and multicultural Other is not a search for an alternative voice with whom the West can engage diplomatically. Nor is it an attempt to correct misrepresentations of the threatening Other by showing amiable Others who speak to the West's cultural values. It is rather a recolonization and repossession of the other—a remaking of the other into the Other after the image of the West.

Misrepresentations of others onscreen are thus more ethically oriented and psychically suggestive of the West's ontological split than we commonly believe. Films with action stars Chuck Norris, Arnold Schwarzenegger, and Clint Eastwood—such as *The Delta Force* (1986), *Commando* (1985), *True Lies* (1994), and *Gran Torino* (2008)—reveal the true status of the Other in the Western eye. In the first three films, all released in the 1980s and early 1990s, the Other directly threatens the symbolic fulcrum of Western society. In these films, the barbaric Other kidnaps innocent people for political or economic gain. And for this reason, in all three films the West responds by dispensing unconditional death to the Other. Eastwood's film provides a contrast. Released in 2008, that is the same year the United States elected its first non-White President, the film shows telltale marks of the changed global times. The other is no longer singularly threatening in a multicultural world. Instead, the non-White incomprehensible foreigner is constitutively split between the good Other and the bad Other, between those who speak English and have embraced American values and those who pidginize the language and corrupt these values through crime. Negotiating a general suspicion of the racial Other with concerns over terrorism and the torture of Guantanamo Bay prisoners, the film adopts a conditional rhetoric of tolerant pluralism. Only those Others who adapt to the American way of life by taking on the American work ethic instead of looting from the community can survive. The dangerous Others are dispensed with. A disgruntled loner and Korean War veteran, Walt Kowalski (Clint Eastwood), does not kill the dangerous Others. Instead, he prompts them to shoot him, dying in a hail of bullets, thereby sacrificing himself Christ-like for the preservation of the American dream. Eastwood's film is a politically correct version of Zack Snyder's *300* (2006). In *300*, Leonidas (Gerard Butler) dies protecting Greek democracy, and the fresco end credit scene shows a dead Leonidas in a Christ-like pose amid the three hundred dead Spartan soldiers. Both films are complicit in organizing knowledge and rehistoricizing popular memory to facilitate the subject formation of the West. The mechanics of subject-production explored in *Orientalism* is not solely dependent on constituting a sovereign self in contrast to a prejudiced image of the Other. The representations of the Other and the sovereign self of the West constituted against that Other are not just products of a racist imaginary. Rather the subjectivity constructed via an other scene categorically establishes the subject of the West as decentered.

Said reads representation as a theatrical act, a performance that is set up in order to constitute Western identity. At one point in the book, Said describes the Orient as a stage on which a theatrical spectacle of the East is presented for Western consumption. This charade enables European imagination to redraw the Orient as an open space. In this empty space, the material reality of the East overlaps with the imagination of

European writers who performatively produce the Orient as an aesthetic simulation—a singular, axiomatic Orient lexicalized to the West. As Said himself puts it,

> The idea of representation is a theatrical one: the Orient is the stage on which the whole East is confined. On this stage will appear figures whose role it is to represent the larger whole from which they emanate. The Orient [is] not an unlimited extension beyond the familiar world, but rather a closed field, a theatrical stage affixed to Europe.[19]

Read in this fashion, *Orientalism* is not merely descriptive of racial power politics and hegemony but also of a fantastic spectacle—the theatricality of constituting the Self via the Other.

It would not be wrong to say that Orientalism describes a fantasy. The steps involved in the process of fantastically constituting colonial reality begin with the identification of the colony as an empty site and the imaginative characterizations of the natives as barbaric and uncivilized. All of these have little to no basis in the real conditions of the colony or its inhabitants. However, the production of the Orient is not simply a matter of imagination and neither is it free from imperial violence. Instead, Orientalism describes the metaphorization of the Orient's mere being—its cultural plurality and the lived reality of its inhabitants substituted by a series of discourses and practices that exclude and displace any actual Orient. It is an Orient arranged, governed, surveyed, secured, and articulated through both direct domination as well as psychic operations that express the colonizer's desire.

This perspective reveals the West as a knowledge-producing subject. But the West remains constitutively decentered, suffering from the anxiety over the lack of any guarantee underwriting the symbolic function of its representations. The Other formed through the negation of the real conditions of the non-European societies remains fragile, and this impels colonial ideology to cover up its gesture of negation and to restrict the real conditions of the colony from rupturing the representations of colonial reality. Physical encounters with colonial reality do not change anything. The phantasmic screen composing of the Other remains intact through direct contact, continuing after the end of colonial occupation and even when the material conditions of the other world may have drastically altered. For example, in the context of India, the rehearsing of the old images of poverty and corruption continue to circulate today just under the image of a global and affluent India. It is interesting to see how Hollywood has acknowledged the globally emergent status of India but kept the "Indian slum" as a constant in its recent productions such as *Slumdog Millionaire*, *Million Dollar Arm*, *Best Exotic Marigold Hotel*, *Eat, Pray, Love*, *Born into Brothels*, and *I Origins*. The message in all these films is clear: yes, India is emerging economically and politically, but it still has the same social problems as before. Eurocentric representations are always caught in a loop. These repeatedly draw the screen of Third World abjection over real conditions of the Third World or the real conditions responsible for Third World poverty in order to conserve the position of Europe as the subject of discourse. By theorizing how European representations function, *Orientalism* leads us to consider the supplementing function of imperial ideology in constructing the fantasy of the Other.

Orientalism shows that imperial ideology functions to overwrite the gap created in the social symbolic by the act of disavowing the otherness of the Other. The gap in the social symbolic marks the absolute lack of communication between two subjects, between the colonizer and the colonized. The Other as an interlocutor is, structurally, always an enigma: we do not understand the Other. The Other is capable of mimicry and sly civility that renders all communication between it and the West ambivalent. Or the subaltern responds with a radical silence that vitiates the West's attempts at knowing the other. These absences in communication between the subject of the West and the other in the non-West are not a matter of language. Learning the other's language cannot bridge the gap that exists between the two. Even with interpreters something is always lost, and this loss is the symptom of an inherent lack structurally bifurcating the colonizer from the colonized. This lack cannot be filled. The native's radical otherness—its cultural plurality and ontological heterogeneity—cannot be overwritten except simplistically, even fantastically, by reducing native others into an Other that necessarily fails to encompass its otherness.

The function of imperial ideology is best understood as aimed at suturing this lack. Only such an act of suture can make the unbearable other disappear and be substituted by a knowable Other. Ideology therefore makes a dialectic interaction between the colonizer and the colonized possible when none actually exists. Serving to bind Europe in a complex communicative relation with the Other, imperial ideology performs the function of *suppléance*. That is to say, it imagines a third, abstract presence in the form of divine right or natural law to symbolically stabilize its representations of, and resulting communications with, the native-Other. Similar to the quark in physics, this ideology seeks to make the colonial social symbolic a cohesive whole, though it should be kept in mind that the supplemental function of ideology does not repair the symbolic cleft. Instead, its need for establishing communication between the colonizer and the native paradoxically enunciates the incompleteness of the symbolic order.

Suppléance questions the master signifiers used in imperial representations of the Other. For example, the use of localized practices of *sati* (widow immolation) and "female circumcision" as metaphoric for the entire native culture is a pure function of imperial ideology as *suppléance*. The attribution of *sati* and similar localized practices to the general culture of the native allowed the constitution of the native as an Other and the imperial subject as invested with the responsibility of colonizing the Other in order to save their brown women from their brown men. Examinations of imperialism and neocolonialism today should focus on the strategic arrangements of domination through misdirection, negation of the other, and the function of ideological *suppléance*. Such a reorientation in postcolonial theoretical analysis would allow a meeting of postcolonial examinations of representation, discursive exercises of power, and formation of subjectivities with the material conditions of unequal distribution of wealth.

Homi Bhabha

Homi Bhabha's work is identified closely with French theory, specifically that of Lacan and Derrida. The concepts of colonial ambivalence, mimicry, and hybridity provide the basis for his thought. Rather than accepting the colonizer–colonized dichotomy, he constantly problematizes it, which gives his theory a different bearing than that of Said, who sees consistency rather than contradiction in the colonizer–colonized relationship.

Bhabha reveals colonialism as a hesitant practice. Imperial authority and the colonized's response to that authority, Bhabha claims, are never stable. These are unnervingly contingent, tirelessly repetitive, and necessarily performative. Bhabha notes in "Signs Taken for Wonders" that "colonial presence is always ambivalent . . . split between its appearance as original and authoritative and its articulation as repetition and difference."[20] This split is the site of contradiction within the colonial discourse itself, contradiction that Said does not address. Similarly, in "The Other Question," Bhabha shows that colonial "knowledge and identification" of the native are continually dithering "between what is always 'in place,' already known, and something that must be anxiously repeated."[21] The European book (the Bible) becomes the prosthesis to imperial rule. While appearing to narrate the success and functionality of the regime, imperial discourse around the book paradoxically enunciates the fragility of the empire. The transfer of authority to an external, material, inanimate object announces the failure of the human as it opens up the colony to the travails of the object as thing. The other riles authority in continuing to exist in an ungenteel and unapologetic form. Gaps that emerge in context of the book's failure to authorize the regime—the gap between imperial desire to know and control and the sheer impossibility of the colony—make the colony ambivalent and arranges native subversion. Anti-colonial resistance surfaces at the interstices of imperial knowing and not knowing.

Bhabha does not only perceive colonial societies as elastic, but postcolonial cultures as well. One finds in his writings an insistence on reading contemporary global conflicts as more than simple binaries, that is, as conflicts between us and them, between Western modernity and Islamofascism. This is the case even when the dichotomy appears intractable. In the context of the *fatwa* surrounding Salman Rushdie's 1988 novel *The Satanic Verses*, Bhabha writes,

> The conflict of cultures and community around *The Satanic Verses* has been mainly presented in spatial terms and binary geopolitical polarities – Islamic fundamentalists vs. Western literary modernists . . . this obscures the anxiety of the irresolvable, borderline culture of hybridity that articulates its problems of identification and its diasporic aesthetic in an uncanny, disjunctive temporality that is, at once, the *time* of cultural displacement, and the *space* of the untranslatable.[22]

The point to be taken from Bhabha is that there is always an unaccounted, unresolved, and untranslatable excess emergent from colonial and postcolonial cultural encounters.

This is why it is not enough to dismiss Bhabha's theories as arcane (as Aijaz Ahmad does) or as responsible for dissolving colonial politics into the play of semiotics (as Benita Parry does). It is also not enough to claim that Bhabha ignores history, that he suspends historical materialism and fails to identify structures of imperial domination and indigenous opposition to it. These objections to his work fail to comprehend the true import of Bhabha's hypotheses of the colonial universe as volatile, phantasmagorical, and in flux. These criticisms also overlook an important aspect of Bhabha's writings on colonial discourse analysis, namely, the native's sly political engagement with the empire. The native abject in the garb of the mimic galvanizes resistance by folding the vernacular nonsense into and, at other times, by abstracting the vernacular nonsense from, colonial discourse. The nonsense lingers, irrevocably, and undoes the imperial reality. What appears in cultural encounters as the symptomatic proof of this excess? Anxiety. Bhabha states this most unequivocally when commenting on our continuous inclination to rephrase all geopolitical conflicts in terms of cultural binaries as serving to obscure an anxiety over encountering what these conflicts expose in the form of an irredeemable remainder of interpersonal exchanges.

To understand Bhabha properly, we must shift our focus to his ideas, however undeveloped they might be, on anxiety.[23] Bhabha reads colonial relationships and imperial discourse as fraught with a sense of dislocating anxiety. Moments of colonial anxiety or political panic expose the fragility of the regime. For Bhabha, anxiety surfaces not in experience, but through acts of representation that translate the contingent into the historical. In other words, anxiety is not outside discourse. It emerges at the interstices of imperial writing designing a discourse of mastery in face of the impossibility of symbolizing the teeming multiplicity of the colony. Unlike Fanon who situates anxiety in experiences of the other, Bhabha identifies its origin in the production of discourse. He reads anxiety as a phenomenon of colonial discourse—an after-effect of constructing a singular imaginary of the Other abstracted from the plural reality of the other's culture. Bhabha sees anxiety inhabiting the colonial space as a fundamental signature that affectively reorders colonial relations, practices, representations, and ideologies.

In his major essays (such as "Articulating the Archaic," "The Other Question," "By Bread Alone," and "Signs Taken for Wonders"), Bhabha speaks about two kinds of anxieties, without noting himself the difference between these two types. First, there is anxiety that surfaces due to the sudden intrusion of radical otherness into the imperial symbolic. This is symbolic anxiety. Second, there is anxiety that surfaces when one encounters the imperial symbolic as lacking. This is real anxiety. These moments are responsible for stretching meaning and identity in colonial discourse toward two different directions: toward the signifier and toward jouissance (or enjoyment). Fantasy negotiates these traumatic encounters with anxiety-provoking native things and the horror of experiencing the imperial symbolic as lacking by erecting a frame for desire.

Consider the example of Adela Quested's traumatic encounter with the abyss of the unknown real in E. M. Forster's novel *A Passage to India* (1924). Early on in the novel, Adela announces her wish to see the real India. Adela wants to see India not through an arranged "Bridge Part," but as it really is. In her quest to discover this real India what she sees is the unspeakable core or the abyss of an ancient land that cannot be represented in speech. She perceives the bowels of the Marabar caves. Yet what appears between her memory and her testimony at court regarding her experience inside the caves is a fantasy—Dr. Aziz, the Indian accompanying Adela on the trip, molested her. This fantasy of the rapist Other discloses the need for experiencing the excess in life, that is, of being fleetingly touched by the Other. Put in the context of the present, this means enjoying the otherness of the Other without allowing this otherness to completely overcome the subject of the West. The West's fascination with the other side of the non-West—*injira* and yoga and quinoa—and not its essential otherness-in-difference illustrates the need for touching the radical otherness of the Other without disturbing the Western subject or the position of the West as subject.

David Lean's film adaptation of Forster's novel captures the thrill and horror of this remarkably well in a scene that is not found in Forster's text. The scene comes last in a series of four significant scenes. The first three in chronological order are: the scene where Dr. Aziz (Victor Banerjee) plans a trip to the Marabar caves; the scene where Adela (Judy Davis) confesses to Ronny Heaslop (Nigel Havers) that she does not want to marry him; and, the rather awkward scene of a dinner table conversation between Ronny and her mother, Adela's travel companion, Mrs. Moore (Peggy Ashcroft), where Mrs. Moore says to Ronny, "sometime I think too much fuss is made about marriage. Century after century of carnal embracement ... and we're still no nearer understanding one another." It is the scene that follows these three that is the most significant for my argument here.

In this scene, as if to escape the stifling possibilities of all the three previous scenes but still possessed of the need to see the real India, Adela journeys out of Chandrapore on a bicycle. The shots showing her leave and travel further away from the city suggest her flight into otherness. We first watch her leave the city framed by a huge curved gateway, and then watch her travel down a tree-lined boulevard further and further into the distance toward a vanishing zero point. Both the shots create a sense of Adela's freedom as she steps away from the city together with a sense of uncertainty in seeing her journey into the native wilderness. In particular the second long shot showing her pedal away from us and toward the horizon creates the initial sense of unease that returns a few shots later when Adela, now about twelve miles away from Chandrapore, comes across some old ruins. In a shot mirroring the shot of her leaving Chandrapore, we see her now enter the ruins framed by yet another open gateway. Beginning with her departure from the modern-day city to her entering the ancient ruins, the shots line up to suggest Adela moving from one perspective to another as well as from one time (British India) to another (pre-colonial India). Once inside, Adela travels through the ruins gazing at statues of the divine and the mortals scattered alike in various stages of decline. But only when she reaches the innermost part of the ruins does she encounter the radical alterity of the Other—stone carvings of human couples in diverse postures of physical intimacy. Close-ups of Adela's face show discomfort and anxious disbelief as she watches with delightful horror a part of real India censored from both imperial and nationalist discourses of the time. But at this very moment a group of monkeys suddenly descend down from the top of the ruins to scare Adela away.

These primates function as *Deus ex machina*—their sudden, chattering intervention into the scene saves Adela from bearing the stress of gazing too intently at the enjoyment of the Other. The creatures cut Adela's agonizing experience short. Adela had set out see the real India. She had set out on a journey into her fantasy, and what she encountered inside that fantasy was the horror of the Other's enjoyment. Caught in the twilight of her fantasy, Adela is reduced to an object bereft of power or privilege (of sight) gazing spellbound at the stone reliefs of the Other's sexual enjoyment. Her need to return to reality, to the stifling conditions of her life set out in the previous three scenes, is imperative. That subjective wretchedness is much better than an encounter with the traumatic core of the Other, yet she is arrested like an animal in the gaze of the Other's lovemaking. Only the monkeys help her escape from the gaze of the Other and back into the world where her subjectivity is restituted as a longing, desiring, suffering subject.

This incident presages the cave incident in Lean's film. It is Lean's brilliance that he thought of this scene because in presaging the cave incident this scene appears to suggest that Adela must make the same mistake twice. In the cave incident as well, Adela appears to have been caught in the desire of the Other. Or what she fantasized as the Other's desire. She is thus a metaphor for the most liberal side of the Empire, which cannot stop its compulsive habit of imagining the Other. The sudden and almost prohibitive restriction of Adela's voyeuristic delight also illustrates the need for the Empire to remain securely distant from coming too close to the Other's otherness. In strict terms, the empire cannot know the Other beyond broad categories of identity and difference. The Other's most intimate practices must be excised in order for the self of the West to claim its high moral and political grounds. Yet, and herein lies the cause of imperial inconsistency over authority, this displaced knowledge insists itself into existence and thereby forces the empire into acknowledging the presence of this traumatic Other through fantasy scenarios.

What animates Bhabha's theorizations of the colony and postcolony in non-binary terms is an emphasis on the dialectic of seeing and looking, of knowing and of not knowing, of the familiar conjoined to the unfamiliar. His essays index an outside of discourse, an intimation of a exegesis unfolding on the obverse of discourse, bringing into adjacency a beyond-of-the-signified that in its vacillation between presence and absence confuses the order of imperial cognition. It is not that the Empire does not know. The Empire is not ignorant; but it wavers due to the vernacular other—the radical alterity of the Other—which remains as evanescent knowledge. The traumatic otherness exists as unacknowledged knowledge, or knowledge that does not know it "by the name of knowledge."[24]

Gayatri Chakravorty Spivak

Gayatri Spivak is often considered the most difficult and the most esoteric of the postcolonial theorists. Much of the problem stems from what critics call Spivak's opaque writing. However, Spivak's writing style has a precise thematic significance: it demonstrates her cautious engagement with language. She does not write to be difficult, but she questions the veracity of simple prose when it comes to writing about difficult subject matters like gendered subalternity. In addition, Spivak attempts to deconstruct her own writing from within the First World academy and stands against the academic practice of building enclosed systems of interpretative narratives.

The best response to criticisms about her writing style has come from Spivak herself. She sees the charge that her writing lacks clarity as part of the way that the First World academy seeks to marginalize the Third World postcolonial theorist. This demand that the postcolonialist write in simple prose is an attempt to domesticate the Third World intellectual as a potential agent of knowledge who otherwise does not fit tidily within the paradigms of the West. The ability of the Third

World intellectual to produce knowledge and interrogate Western production of knowledge receives a cold reception in the First World academy.

The Third World postcolonial critic in the First World university is at once a familiar yet unfamiliar figure. Critics use various labels to describe Spivak and her work. However none of these, including the broad label "feminist Marxist deconstructivist," has succeeded in capturing Spivak's intellectual range or her radical theoretical interventions into sacred European epistemic configurations. Much of the academy's discomfort with Spivak has to do with her radical undecidability—her fleeting presence in and persistent critique of all theoretical habitus. For instance, speaking to Elizabeth Grosz, Spivak characterizes the disciplines of "feminism," "Marxism," and "deconstruction" as inveterately marked by "colonialist influence."[25] She explains her continual traversing of these disciplinary spaces as aimed at positing these in tension to one another. The job of the postcolonial theorist is to inhabit these systems of thinking and employing these systems to think about cultural politics without forgetting to tirelessly interrupt these disciplinarian discourses.

An excellent illustration of this interruptive practice is found in Spivak's 1985 essay "Three Women's Texts and a Critique of Imperialism." In this essay, Spivak notes how Charlotte Bronte's *Jane Eyre* constitutes Jane as a new feminine idea by killing off Rochester's creole wife Bertha Mason. In the novel, Bertha is presented as a mad woman confined in Rochester's attic. She later dies in a fire that she had started in a fit of madness, thereby clearing the way for Jane's marriage to Rochester. To Spivak, Bertha is a represented subject whose voice is absent in the narrative, lost in her ranting, and her accidental death legitimizes Jane's social ascension through marriage. Feminist scholarship celebrated Jane as a model of independent female subjectivity, conveniently overlooking Bronte's treatment of Bertha as a racialized Other. This has not only meant the diminution of Bertha to the status of a minor narrative device, but also an erasure of the novel's connection to race and the empire. The subject-production of Jane depends on the presence in absence of Bertha, and by extension, the colony and the Other. But these presences never materialize in the novel as coerced sites of imperial enterprise. Rather, the Other exists in a way that represses its real status in the empire and the colony is conjoined to the service of the imperial nation as it embarks on constituting new subject formations suitable to the new social politics of an imperial age. And although we remain unconcerned about this Other, the reader's enjoyment over and the narrative building of Jane's character rests on the fetishized presence of the Other. The colony and the native are commodities in the Marxist sense of the term—the value of the fetishized Other is more than its worth in exploited resources and labor as the Other facilitates the West's production of knowledge and subjectivity. Academic scholarship celebrating Jane's subjectivity therefore contributed to the cultural production of the novel's meaning by perpetuating another act of disavowal. The postcolonial intervention is thus not limited to Bronte's textual politics only; rather, it extends to unravel the academic sanction of Jane's subject formation. Jane is doubly inscribed and the subaltern's excision doubly rehearsed. And because she identifies the subaltern in and through these moments of erasure, Spivak challenges the usual conceptions of identity and difference.

Perhaps the most famous of Spivak's interruptions has been her intercession into Foucault and Deleuze's conversation on the topic of capital and third world labor. In what is probably her most famous essay, "Can the Subaltern Speak?," Spivak intercedes in an exclusively white, European, male conversation about the marginalized.[26] The essay is the occasion for a powerful critique of systematic excision of subaltern voices in dominant discourses. "Can the Subaltern Speak?" demonstrates how even the most politically radical discourses end up consolidating the position of the West as the Subject and subject of that discourse. The subaltern functioning only to give better contrast to arguments already deemed universal.

It is not only Western intellectuals like Foucault and Deleuze who are unknowingly complicit in the processes of silencing the Third-World-gendered subaltern. Spivak's criticism extends as well to the Subaltern Studies collective and their failure to consider the gender question in relation to the subcontinental subaltern. In fact, Spivak is adamant on the point that any representation of the subaltern from the outside is tantamount to silencing the subaltern. For not only do such representations dissolve the heterogeneity of subaltern identity and community, the proscription of a singular cultural identity to the subaltern merely reinscribes the latter into the repressive apparatus of the prevailing social symbolic order. Bereft of the language with which to self-represent and in the absence of any access to modes of self-representation, the subaltern remains spoken for—and hence silenced.

The subaltern as limit

Spivak chooses the term "subaltern" carefully. Though it seems like a perfect instance of needless complexity and jargon, Spivak insists that "subaltern" is not a "classy word for [the] oppressed." It is not a blanket term for the oppressed, as it does not apply to the urban "working class" or to "a discriminated-against minority on the university campus." The subaltern is a term reserved for those outside of and without access to "the hegemonic discourse."[27] As Spivak sees it, none of the other available terms readily indicate this position.

Spivak's subaltern is a radical limit that constitutively marks the incapacity of Western representation to symbolize—to read or listen to—those who have no stake in its discourse. The subaltern definitely talks, but the subaltern does not speak. We hear the subaltern but do not listen to her. The subaltern is not outside the social, the visual, and the nomenclatural. It is marked by its "position without identity."[28] That is to say, the subaltern has a position in society—it votes, figures in the census, is part of government and NGO relief data—but it has no identity. Unable to represent itself or participate in the process of representation, the subaltern remains barred from procuring identity. Any form of representation involves a political othering of the Other. The subaltern exists in a position tangential to this process. Therefore, any attempt to answer the question, "What does the subaltern want?," is complicit in putting subalternity into crisis. One cannot answer this question without speaking for or on behalf of the subaltern. Constituted by an "immense discontinuous network of political ideology, economics, history, sexuality, language," the subaltern remains outside and/or indifferent to the mainstream.[29] It exists adjacent to, yet remains different from, the universal. In other words, the subaltern falls outside of epistemic totalizations to expose Western knowledge as violent and self-gratifying. Inhabiting a position beyond enunciation, it is barred in relation to the symbolic order (as constitutional excess) and, when allowed into the symbolic it either interrupts or is folded into the Other (as in the dialogue between Foucault and Deleuze).

Most specifically, the subaltern inhabits the beyond of discourse because it marks the impassibility of enunciation within a singular sign system inscribed by impossibility of alternatives. This singularity of Western knowledge is constituted more by what is structurally excluded than included. Claiming a vocabulary for and on behalf of the excised subaltern is a fantasy of which the Western intellectual is implicitly guilty. As Veena Das observes, the subaltern forces us to rethink Europe's relation with the rest of the world "from a point of view that displaces the central position of [Europe] as the subject of discourse and [the Other] as its object."[30] An unreadable epistemic and political signature, the subaltern haunts the nominative through evading, challenging, staining, and disrupting the logic, time, and performance of what is. That is to say, the subaltern appears as an affective absence or silence that introduces the heterogeneously fractured other.

The subaltern in the symbolic appears as an anamorphic blot, an ungraspable enigma, whose speech does not reach us. Like the apparition in Pedro Almodovar's film *The Devils' Backbone* (2001), we see the subaltern moving its lips but we cannot hear any of the words coming out from her mouth. This is not because we do not comprehend the language of the other, but the other might not be addressing its speech to us at all. The other might not see us, and even if it does it might not register our being-in-nakedness, very much like the cat that Jacques Derrida describes in *The Animal That Therefore I Am*. According to Derrida, his cat sees him naked and marks his nakedness, but it can never speak this nakedness. Derrida's own shame is registered even though there is no signification attached to the act of registering it (because it is a cat and not a speaking being).[31] The existence of the subaltern in the social symbolic order is a painful reminder of our subjective limitations. It is vis-à-vis its nonexistent presence that ontological experiences can appear empty, grand narratives hollow, and subjectivity abject.

Postcolonial film theory does not exist

When turning from postcolonial theory to postcolonial film theory, one notices first a massive lacuna. Properly speaking, there is no such thing as postcolonial film theory. This does not mean there are no postcolonial films or works of postcolonial film criticism. One could easily say that films about colonialism and its aftermath or films made by filmmakers from former colonized countries can all be defined as postcolonial cinema. The category can include films as diverse as Michael Haneke's *Caché* (2005), Gillo Pontecorvo's *Queimada* (1969), David Lean's *A Passage to India* (1984), Satyajit Ray's *Panter Panchali* (1955), Ousmane Sembène's *Xala* (1975), and, Philip Kaufman's *Rising Sun* (1993). The categories of national, transnational, intercultural, accented, exilic, and diasporic films can also be part of this broad nomination. Similarly, critical examinations of films from a postcolonial perspective can be identified as pursuing postcolonial film criticism. The writings of Robert Stam, Ella Shohat, Louis Spence, Teshome Gabriel, Sara Ahmed, Kin-Yan Szeto, Madhava Prasad, and Reena Dube on films as different from one another as *The Birth of a Nation* (1915), *Xala* (1975), *Bend it like Beckham* (2002), *Taste of Cherry* (1997), *Roja* (1992), *Lust, Caution* (2007), and *Satranj Ke Khiladi* (1977) bear witness to substantial efforts toward interrogating cinema in the contexts of colonial, decolonial, and neocolonial histories. Interrogating issues of race, multiculturalism, Third Cinema, hegemony, and representational politics that include aspects of otherness unregistered in mainstream films and film criticisms, these works accentuate the diverse modalities through which films over the years have illustrated, challenged, excised, and negotiated the history of colonialism and its multiple aftermaths.

The existence of postcolonial cinema and postcolonial criticism of cinema is therefore beyond question. What is absent, however, is a distinguishable theoretical framework that examines cinema in relation to the pre-filmic referent of the empire and that defines a specifically postcolonial approach to film. In this sense, there is no postcolonial film theory in the way that there is feminist film theory or psychoanalytic film theory. As a result, one must assemble it piecemeal by bringing together the various approaches and by examining how the fundamental tenets of postcolonial theory explored above can be brought to bear on the cinema.

Susan Hayward's entry on "postcolonial theory of film" in *Cinema Studies: The Key Concepts* (2012) and Robert Stam's discussion of "Film and the Postcolonial" in *Film Theory: An Introduction* (2000) offer good illustrations of the absence of any postcolonial film theory. Hayward's entry is not even a stand-alone entry on postcolonial film theory. Instead, rather symptomatically, it is appended to her entry on "postcolonial theory." I will cite part of this entry at length because it shows the most common and characteristic direction of thinking about the use of postcolonial theory in analysis of films.

Hayward writes,

> Postcolonial theory when applied to cinema studies helps us read (through a non-Eurocentric eye, hopefully) films

> emanating from postcolonial/post-colonial countries as well as films from the diaspora. These films, which explore questions of representation, identity and location politics (i.e. who is the speaking subject and where is s/he speaking from?), also question the center/margin binaries imposed by Western thought. Models of colonialist discourse are exposed, as are the practices of dependency theory (the way in which global capitalism functions to maintain the impoverishment of the economically colonized developing world). The legacy of the exploitation of the colonized body is explained through a demonstration of how the diasporic movements, generated by slavery, are later matched by the ecological imperialism of the formerly colonizing nations. . . . But, this is not the only cinema that postcolonial theory examines. It is used also to analyze films made by the West – both during colonialist era and in the postcolonial moment – which either directly or indirectly display their Eurocentrism.[32]

While Hayward admirably tries to describe a vision of postcolonial film theory that holds together, even a cursory look at this account shows that it does not. There are at least three basic problems in this short entry.

First, Hayward limits the application of the postcolonial optics to only "films emanating from postcolonial/post-colonial countries." The question is: what are these countries? Should postcolonial analysis apply only to films from formerly colonized countries in Asia, Africa, and South America? If yes, then, her taxonomy suffers from a serious lacuna because it overlooks the impact of imperialism on certain communities in Europe itself (the Roma in France), settler colonies (Australia), and nations not directly colonized (China).

Second, there is a general lack of clarity in Hayward's entry about the term "postcolonial." This makes any attempt to devise or derive therefrom a postcolonial theory of film extremely difficult. It is not clear whether postcolonial refers primarily to the object of study (a postcolonial region) or to an approach toward any object (postcolonial theory as a theory). Perhaps Hayward is attempting to capture this difference in her use of the term "postcolonial" in both a hyphenated and non-hyphenated way. In any event, one must be clear what postcolonial refers to.

Third, there is no attempt to distinguish postcolonial film theory from postcolonial theory as such. Hayward never describes the specific difference that constitutes postcolonial film theory or how it responds to medium specificity. A film theory must take the filmic medium into account, and postcolonial theory is rooted not in a visual medium but in a written one. Clearly, a theory derived to address issues of postcoloniality in film will exist in relation to postcolonial theory. But it must be distinct as well, keeping in mind the generic, stylistic, and technological arrangements of cinema.

But Hayward is not the only case where we see a lack of theoretical rigor when it comes to thinking about a framework suitable to the study of postcolonial cinema. Robert Stam's *Film Theory: An Introduction*, while offering brilliantly detailed overviews of major film theories and their corollaries, cannot do so when it comes to postcolonial film theory. Ironically, Stam emphasizes the importance of postcolonial analysis of films very strongly in both the preface and the introduction to the book. In the introduction, for example, Stam deplores the failure of cinema scholars to historically situate film and film theory in relation to imperialism. Yet his chapter on "Film and the Postcolonial" is only a brief six and a half pages. That is less than 2 percent of a book that spends much of its preface and introduction decrying the absence of postcolonial film theory. To be fair to Stam, if we include his chapters on Third Cinema and Third World theory and "Multiculturalism, Race, and Representation," then he has a total of forty pages or about 10 percent of the book dealing with the postcolonial in the very broadest terms.

But the larger problem is that Stam's section on postcolonial film theory offers nothing more than outlines of the positions of Edward Said, Homi Bhabha, and Gayatri Spivak without seeking to extend these discussions toward a hypothesis on postcolonial film theory. Furthermore, when we compile the three sections together what becomes evident is the traditional European narrative of Othering the other: each chapter isolates theories of otherness and difference as most appropriate for analyzing non-European films. While European and American films claim universal apertures such as auteurship, narratology, and psychoanalysis, the films of the Other matter for their difference. The latter must allegorically enunciate their nationalist ontologies and cultural peculiarities for the appreciation of the masses in the West. The intellectual vacillation of Stam comes to the fore when he writes in the section on Third Cinema that it is primarily due to First World assumptions that non-European films "only express 'local' concerns [that] this body of work was rarely seen as forming part of the history of 'universal'" film theory.[33] But Stam's own reading of postcolonial cinema a few pages before suffers from the same unconscious assumption.

It would be unjust to say that the usefulness of postcolonial film theory for examining the representational practice of Western films is completely missing from Hayward's or Stam's account. Hayward, for instance, makes a cursory but useful comment at the very end of her entry. She writes, "[postcolonial theory] is used also to analyze films made by the West – both during colonialist era and in the postcolonial moment – which either directly or indirectly display their Eurocentrism."[34] In other words, postcolonial theory is useful for interrogating the production, circulation, and dissemination of Eurocentric images of the Other in Western cultural discourses. But in the end, this is yet another way of localizing the theory in terms of historicity and assessing its methodology as valuable only in the context of a specific historical referent. Yes, postcolonial theory and postcolonial film theory must acknowledge the history of the empire as an important pre-filmic referent, but that alone cannot validate its critical methodology and nor can the said methodology be limited to explorations of the West's stereotypical representations of the non-West. The structural relegation of the West to the end of Hayward's entry is actually connected to this ideological bent. By coming at the end of an entry on postcolonial film theory, it appears in the text almost as an afterthought and suggests the relative lack of importance of this particular point. By comparison, all that comes before establishing a direct association between the postcolonial and the non-Western Other gains weight. As is the case with Stam, Hayward's entry identifies the postcolonial with the non-West and as a critical methodology valid only for exploring the experiences and the histories of the Other with the West remaining a self-reflexive universal. This move forestalls the reach of postcolonial film theory by preventing the indispensable task of interrogating the West's complicity in production of knowledge and subjectivity.

Hayward also limits the analytic scope of postcolonial film theory. For her, postcolonial film theory identifies direct and indirect displays of Eurocentrism. But such analyses have a limited use in the current global capitalist universe with its growing sensitivity to cultural difference. Of course, continuing imperial wars and the rise of political conservatism in Europe on issues of immigration make analysis of existing modalities of Eurocentrism vital. But the problem is the focus on representation. The question today is no longer what is represented (the non-West as x or y), but rather how racial discourse and colonial expressions continue to circulate surreptitiously clothed in and legitimized as neoliberal rhetoric. It is important to unravel how politically correct images of the Other are used to conserve and support the subject of the West. The focus of analysis, as such, needs to free itself from the straightjacket of the critique of representation and focus on the production of the West as a knowledge/subject-producing subject (which also provides medium specificity for postcolonial film theory, since this production occurs most forcefully in the cinema).

What is at stake is the dismantling of realities produced by cinema in the West. Let us take a random example, James Cameron's 1997 film *Titanic*. Though there are no direct representational references to the non-European Other, the material object of the ship might be contextualized in a history of imperial production to ask questions about the relation between colonial labor and industrial manufacture in Britain. This theoretical gesture is essential to a postcolonial film theory that is prepared to address all types of films rather than finding itself relegated to particular cases in Western cinema where the Other is overtly present. We need to start considering the usefulness of expanding the meaning of the term postcolonial in context of global cinema in the twenty-first century alongside rearranging the analytic scope of the theory to include films otherwise not considered valid objects of postcolonial study.

Three recent books have already argued for this need and taken some steps toward reconceptualizing the field of postcolonial cinema. These are Elizabeth Heffelfinge and Laura Wright's *Visual Difference: Postcolonial Studies and Intercultural Cinema* (2011), Sandra Ponzanesi and Marguerite Waller's *Postcolonial Cinema Studies* (2012), and Rebecca Weaver-Hightower and Peter Hulme's *Postcolonial Film: History, Empire, Resistance* (2014).[35] While the specific arguments of each book differ, at a more general level all three underscore the need to reimagine and retool postcolonial film theory to look beyond interrogating the issues of race, empire, national politics, and diaspora. To this end, they propose expanding the field of postcolonial cinema by including all cinemas as the postcolonial subject matter. More specifically, they look at films, irrespective of their geographic provenance, that are either complicit with or resistant to imperial and neocolonial regimes, as well as films whose formation bespeaks the technologies and the economic condition of the global present. Along with this expansion of the scope of postcolonial film analysis, they urge renewing a multifaceted dialogue between cinema studies and postcolonial theory.

Taking a cue from and seeking to contribute to these conversations about postcolonial film theory, I focus in the remaining part of this chapter on starting a conversation around the possibility of imagining a genealogy of and thematization for postcolonial film theory through Third Cinema. In what follows, I do not propose to build or even propose a comprehensive theoretical framework. In fact, my postcolonial skepticism over such system-building exercises is partly responsible for the direction my discussion takes in the following pages. Instead of trying to build a normative category for postcolonial film theory, therefore, I prefer to sketch out select viewpoints drawn from postcolonial theory and Third Cinema in order to begin the process of charting a theory of postcolonial analysis of cinema.

While engagement with postcolonial theory is natural in the context of a discussion of postcolonial film theory, bringing up Third Cinema is not. In one sense, a return to the Third Cinema movement in the twenty-first century seems anachronistic given the demise of the Third World movement and the inclination of nation states today to strategically denationalize state sovereignty. Nonetheless, we will focus on Third Cinema because most critics (including Robert Stam) acknowledge it as the logical precursor of postcolonial cinema. I believe the theoretical dimensions of the Third Cinema movement, especially its derivation from the thought of Frantz Fanon and its emphasis on oppositional politics, will work toward conceptualizing some of the principles of postcolonial film theory. There are at least two critical vectors in the Third Cinema movement that will benefit postcolonial film theory. The first one is the Third Cinema movement's interrogation of cinematic rules and narrative realities as constitutively affiliated to Western knowledge systems. Second, postcolonial film theory must embrace Third Cinema movement's emphasis on dismantling the West's production of consumable and consumer realties through narratives that satisfy audience expectations. Both these principles of analysis should be incorporated into postcolonial film theory for interrogating the current modalities through which First World cinema continues to dispossess and repossess the non-West.

Reading Third Cinema postcolonially

The Third Cinema movement began as an aesthetic and political project guiding filmmakers from Africa, Asia, and Latin America during the politically charged period of the 1960s. The three decades following the end of World War II were marked by a series of epochal events. On the one hand, the rapid decolonization of the globe following the collapse of the British and other European empires occurred, and, on the other, a parsing out of the world's territories between the Soviet Union and the United States in the aftermath of the defeat of the Axis alliance took place. Tied to these phenomena were the revolutionary struggles in Cuba, China, Algeria, and Vietnam; the civil rights struggle in the United States; student movements in Paris, Berkeley, and Calcutta; the emergence of state socialism in varying degrees in non-aligned countries (including Egypt, Yugoslavia, Ghana, and India); and the growing popularity of armed Maoist insurrections in different parts of the global South. These historical impulses contributed to the birth of the Third Cinema movement, which sought to extend the radical political beliefs of the time to filmmaking and other forms of art.

The movement emerged in response to the inequalities prevailing between Europe and its former colonies. Proponents of Third Cinema identified these inequalities as resulting from years of colonial exploitation and the continuing extortions of the recently decolonized nations by Europe's neocolonial policies. For its aesthetics, Third Cinema drew inspiration from *Cinema Novo* in Brazil, especially the work of Glauber Rocha in "The Aesthetic of Hunger" (1965), as well as Italian Neorealism and French New Wave. Marx and the Marxist writings of Che Guevara and Mao Tse Dung, along with the anti-colonial works of Frantz Fanon, inspired the philosophy of radical emancipation that formed the philosophical basis for Third Cinema. According to its earliest proponents, the Argentinian filmmakers Fernando Solanas and (the Spanish-born) Octavio Getino, Third Cinema was the expression of Third World's impulse toward emancipation from colonialism, imperialism, and neocolonialism.[36]

The term "Third Cinema" comes from Solanas and Getino's manifesto *Hacia un tercet cine* or *Towards a Third Cinema*. Published in 1969, a year after the release of their film *La Hora de los hornos* [*Hour of Furnaces*], the Third Cinema manifesto theorized the main currents of a third way of filmmaking. It defined this third way as militant, political, and experimental in contrast to and in opposition of North American and European filmic conventions. A year before, while working on their film, Solanas and Getino had already tried out many of the principles they propose in the manifesto. They consciously constructed their film as an independent and militant work that would employ an experimental film language aimed at thwarting the traditional film language of the West.

Third Cinema names two forms of cinema that it constitutes itself in juxtaposition with. These are First Cinema or mainstream Hollywood cinema and Second Cinema or European art house film and auteurist cinema. As first and foremost a political cinema, it opposes the economic and imaginative strangleholds exerted by traditional, mainstream cinemas of the West. That is to say, it contests First World's distribution circuits and the onscreen realities promoted by First and Second Cinemas, realities that often caricature Third World culture and history.

It is important to remember that First Cinema and Second Cinema do not index geographical provenance. First Cinema is not strictly correlative to American cinema or Hollywood, and Second Cinema is not strictly correlative to European cinema or just French cinema. These terms describe films that are stylistically and thematically complicit with capitalist modes of production and social organization with no particular concern for the Third World. But not all films produced in the United States fit this description, just as not every European film is a form of auteur driven cinema. Similarly, national cinema in the Third World can be and often are complicit with the dynamics of global capitalism and blithely unconcerned about the real conditions of the Third World masses.

Solanas and Getino describe Third Cinema as a historical necessity ushered in by the political situations of decolonization, neo-imperial territorial wars, and the revolutionary struggles in Latin American countries. In the face of this history, the task of the Third-World filmmaker is three-fold: (1) To inspire revolutionary ideals in the masses and to lead them toward heightened political consciousness; (2) to subvert cinematic codes mandated by establishment cinema; and (3) to embrace counter-hegemonic ideals to combat the passive filmgoing experience of commercial cinema, thereby rescuing audiences from becoming docile consumers. In this way, Solanas and Getino theorize Third Cinema as a form of resistance against the European colonization of Third World culture, taste, and subjective consciousness.

It is evident from Solanas and Getino's manifesto that they wished Third Cinema to function as an intervention—to be militant, revolutionary, and activist cinema. The third way of filmmaking was to intervene into political situations to begin the process of decolonization of Third World culture. Central to their vision therefore is the call to counter traditional cinema of characters with a cinema of themes, to replace films about individuals with those about people, and to exchange the auteur for an operative group. They believe that these steps could make audiences aware about the form, content, and frameworks of neocolonial misinformation promoted by Hollywood cinema that constitute the Third World as markets of docile consumption.

The real politics of this type of cinema lies in its establishment of an open relationship between viewers and the film. It is cinema that intervenes and provokes, but it is also an unfinished, open-ended work in progress. Just as some creative writers from former colonized countries appropriated the colonizer's language to write back against the colonizer, so too did proponents of Third Cinema. They dismantled habitual identification of cinema as screen by opening up the process of filmmaking and by reconceptualizing cinema—even spectatorship—as an act to liberate representation from the hegemony of neocolonial forces. Third Cinema aimed to decolonize Third World cultures through a repoliticization of these hitherto colonized cultures.

Third Cinema in the university I: from manifesto to methodology

Teshome Gabriel is one of the first scholars to formalize a theory of and organize a methodology for studying Third Cinema. In the course of his long academic career, Gabriel updated and revised his theories, sometimes parting from the manifestos of the 1960s and sometimes drawing out arguments contained in these manifestos in greater relief. His views on the subject consequently offer a more expansive understanding of Third Cinema and enable a formulization of postcolonial film theory in relation to and in the context of it. Gabriel's two most important contributions are his three-part genealogy of Third Cinema and his emphasis on critically understanding the use of oral cultures, cyclical histories, and popular memory in Third Cinema.

Through *Third Cinema in the Third World: The Aesthetics of Liberation* (1982) and essays like "Towards a Critical Theory of Third World Films" (1985) and "Third Cinema as Guardian of Popular Memory: Towards a Third Aesthetics" (1989), Gabriel sketches a three-part genealogy of Third Cinema. It begins with Third Cinema's initial unqualified imitation of Hollywood, then its antithetical phase of remembering purportedly lost indigenous traditions, and, finally, its emergence as a cinema of the masses. It is in this final or combative phase in which Third Cinema truly achieves a complete cultural, psychological, and politico-economic liberation from the West.[37]

Gabriel's genealogical schema situates and defines Third Cinema relationally. For him, Third Cinema exists only in relation to Hollywood. As a result, Gabriel's genealogy ends up portraying Third Cinema as perpetually bound up with the identity of First Cinema. Third Cinema's struggle to break free from the shackles of European and American filmic conventions thus seem like the an unfolding of an Oedipal struggle in which the child attempts to slay the father. But most importantly, a relational definition raises the question of whether or not the political stance of Third Cinema has grown obsolete in the current climate of globalization and new media.

Gabriel himself was all too aware of these limitations, which is why he sought later in his life to update the definition of Third Cinema. In "Third Cinema Updated" he writes, "Third Cinema can no longer be defined [in an era of a rapidly globalizing world] solely in terms of its radical beginnings, its ancestry."[38] Relational politics reductively tethers Third Cinema to the West, whereby the latter remains the primary referent in the binary structure arranging all modes of enunciation including the articulations of dissent. To define Third Cinema only in terms of its initial point of departure marks a failure to see its historical evolution, as Gabriel comes to see. As he takes this evolution into account, Gabriel recognizes that globalization is another form of imperialism but claims that this changed world has not made Third Cinema irrelevant or redundant. The changed world of the twenty-first century may appear to demand a renunciation of the politics of Third Cinema, yet this politics remain crucially pertinent in an age in which global capitalism reigns unchallenged and a reimagined binary of us versus them—those who endorse globalized, nonviolent, multicultural societies and those who pose a threat to this tolerant worldview with revivalist ethno-nationalist and theological fascisms—remains in force. While the politics of interrogating the spread and legitimization of global capital is important, Gabriel advocates for changing the entrenched oppositional stance of Third Cinema. In the face of globalization, the old mode of oppositional politics in cinema becomes problematic. With a ubiquitous though non-repressive capitalist control of life and society becoming a universal reality, the voices of opposition become conjoined to the figure of the terrorists. In this way, ironically, a hardened political opposition ends up serving the structure of global capitalism. As Gabriel puts it, "Global capitalism requires an other, an enemy, in order to constitute itself as universal and homogeneous. . . . To the extent that Third Cinema continues to espouse the rhetoric and thinking of its early days, it is fighting with a phantom that gains strength from every opposition. Hence, Third Cinema becomes not an alternative to Hollywood or capitalism, but merely its mirror, its other."[39] Gabriel calls for replacing the template of oppositional politics with what he calls "composite politics," a structure in which the focus is not on opposition but examining affiliation. He believes a reimagination of a more pragmatic form of politics is the need of the hour. The political revision he demands is consequently expansive and in tune with the revision colonialism has itself undergone over the years to transform into globalization. The reimagined politics of Third Cinema or postcolonial cinema has to be the politics of cunning disorganization of the structures upon which the force of globalization and its novel forms of oppression are shored.

What is this politics of disorganization? And what role can postcolonial film theory play in unraveling textual gestures that rehearse neocolonial politics? Gabriel argues that Third Cinema scholars should not restrict their critique of European and American cinema to the discriminatory representations of the non-West in these films. Neither should these critics celebrate when a Third World film with a more truthful representation of the postcolony is screened in a American theater and applauded by the mainstream press. Rather Third Cinema scholars and filmmakers alike need to disturb the West's appetite for the exotic Other by representing images of otherness that are unassimilable in the cognitive and epistemic systems of the West. Gabriel's argument here builds on Getino and Solanas's manifesto, especially their call to make "*films that the System cannot assimilate and which are foreign to its needs . . . films that directly and explicitly set out to fight the*

System."[40] The role of the Third Cinema or postcolonial scholar should be to accentuate the outsiderly and outlier character of Third Cinema and interpretatively vex hegemonic cinema by drawing out inconsistencies and outlying moments from its narrative to constitutively dismantle the ideological orientation of the narrative.

In "Towards a Critical Theory of Third World Films," Gabriel gives a useful illustration of his point. He notes how Third World cultural contexts and desires for historical signification are often lost to the West. Glauber Rocha's film *Der Leone Have Sept Cabezas* [*The Lion Has Seven Heads*] (1970), for instance, he says, was reviewed in the West as "an allegorical farce noting the bond between Africa and Brazil." But Rocha, on being asked about the subject matter of his film, said it was about "the continuity of the Third World's anti-imperialist struggle from Che to Cabral (and beyond)."[41] Cautious as he is of the pitfalls of historicizing the multi-faceted nature of the Third World movement, Gabriel nonetheless presents Rocha's case to illustrate the limit of Western imagination. He believes that it is the responsibility of the Third World intellectual to expose the gaps and absences in the West's cognitive and symbolic systems of knowledge. Unregimented by the linear logic of causality and time, while accommodating the irrational, the magical, the oral, and the folkloric, Third Cinema is an alternative to the West's realist regime. The act of making Third Cinema is therefore an act of manufacturing an instrument to wrest the power of signification from the West; it is an act of claiming power to write the postcolony in one's own terms.[42] Third Cinema and postcolonial theory disrupt and rearrange the West's positive as well as negative representations of the non-West to show both as tied to acts of self-representation.

It is possible to compare Gabriel's theorizations of Third Cinema with Said's theory of Orientalism. Both advocate the need to retrieve and to reclaim from the West the power to correctively reimagine the symbolic space of the non-West. Both are concerned about unraveling the processes through which Europe stripped the Third World's powers of imagination, language, and signification. Both also appear to share the view that the duty of the Third World intellectual, the filmmaker, and the theorist alike, is to excavate and recuperate from the West's corrupt imaginations the real native, their indigenous traditions, and overlooked popular memories. The purpose is not only to reconvene these on screen or through the written word so as to return to the natives their right to self-represent, but also to destabilize the symbolic edifices of Western knowledge apparatus and breach the cultural production of meaning.

Third Cinema in the university II: Paul Willemen on Third Cinema

One way that university discourse legitimizes hegemony is by accommodating dissenting voices within its bounds. The political interests of the West necessarily undergird university knowledge. Knowledge produced at the university is not neutral and objective but inadvertently complicit in the cultural production of the non-Western Other. We can see a case of this in Paul Willemen's well-known essay on Third Cinema titled "The Third Cinema Question: Notes and Reflections."[43] This essay blunts the edge of Third Cinema politics by qualifying dissent and folding otherness into the discourse of the West.

On one level, Willemen's essay provides an excellent summary review of the seminal features of Third Cinema. He explains the relation of Third Cinema to the Third World, elaborates on the open-ended and unfinished structure of Third Cinema, and notes the exclusion of Third Cinema from the mainstream. But on another level, Willemen's essay is an exercise in bowdlerization. For it approximates and overwrites the most radical perspectives of the Third Cinema movement to present it as not opposed to but as an expedient for Europe's self-appreciation.

Willemen says that Third Cinema is another way to approach cultural politics. He describes it as an attempt by artists and intellectuals to make themselves and their position intelligible. More interestingly, he contends that Third Cinema can help the First World in two specific ways. First, it can change the film culture of the West, and, second, it can enable Britain to cope with the otherness that presents a contemporary challenge to the British worldview. In other words, Third Cinema becomes useful for negotiating the traffic of colored bodies and otherness into post-imperial Britain. Britain, in itself, remains fixed at the center of Willemen's discourse. It is the subject of Willemen's discourse (in both senses of the term "subject"). Third Cinema presents yet another opportunity to recalibrate the centrality of British culture now under stress from the influx of immigrants. But in order to achieve this end, Third Cinema must be thoroughly expunged of its revolutionary vision. It is thus presented as a weak self-aggrandizing project pursued by Third World filmmakers wanting to succeed in the First World (which recalls precisely the allegations against the Third World postcolonial critic in the Anglo-American academy). Third Cinema is captured in an orbit around British society, and the celestial field of British cultural studies, to aid Britain's much-required conscious rebooting of its subjectivity in the post-colonial world.

Marginalizing the confrontational rhetoric of the Third Cinema manifesto, Willemen dismisses Solanas and Getino's document as utopian and as built on previously existing European traditions, examples, and antecedents. He identifies First World (and some Soviet) filmmakers, intellectuals, and cinematic movements as the ideological progenitors of Third Cinema, while de-emphasizing the influence of Third World revolutionaries and revolutionary writings.

Furthermore, in Willemen's reinterpretation of Third Cinema's political agenda, the main thrust shifts from an impulse for emancipation to historical lucidity. Third Cinema mutates from being a provocative interventional cinema that dismantles the

West's representational politics to being an enclosed self-referential system of cinema highlighting conditions of the newly decolonized nation states. In other words, Third Cinema is national cinema.[44] At first glance, it appears that Willemen is keen about preserving the peculiarities of Third Cinema. However, his marking out of Third Cinema as national allegory actually accomplishes the opposite. The codification of Third World cultures as nationalist arrests the non-West in a space specifically designed for it and distant from the center, thereby foreclosing the possibility of encountering the non-West as constitutive of the West. In response to Willemen's account, the question to be asked is, "Why do all Third World projects have to strive for the 'national' when Europe can be, and already always is, universal?" The West wants Third Cinema to fit its regimented vision of historical causality—a narrative with origin and a telos, and filled in with dramatic imaginations of loss and apocalyptic fantasies of retrievals of that loss. But the aim of Third Cinema—and the aim of postcolonial theory, which is the source of the fundamental link between the two—has always been to dismantle such ritualistic processes of thinking. The expectation that Third World cultural texts should always allegorize their nationalist narrative is a Eurocentric attitude. Yet criticisms of such symptomatic enunciations from within the academy are rare, if not absent, and, when present, are overtly cautious. "Perhaps," writes Stam, "because of an assumption that Third World intellectuals could only express 'local' concerns, or because their essays were so overtly political and programmatic, [that] this body of work was rarely seen as forming part of the history of 'universal' – read Eurocentric – film theory."[45] Stam's analysis is correct, but its conclusion is too halting.

It comes as no surprise that Willemen is most distraught with Gabriel's supposed disregard for the category of the nation state in the latter's writings about Third Cinema. He criticizes Gabriel's internationalization of the Third Cinema movement as making the mistake of ignoring the nationalist question, and complains that such thinking compromises the particular Third World situations for an imagined universal ideal of Third World subjectivity. It must be clarified, first, that Gabriel's writings actually offer two different perspectives on the issue. It is true that in his "Towards a Critical Theory of Third World Films," Gabriel makes a direct correlation between Third Cinema and the Third World. However, in the book *Third Cinema in the Third World* (1982) and in the essay "Third Cinema as Guardian of Popular Memory: Towards a Third Aesthetics," Gabriel makes no equivocal connection between Third Cinema and the Third World. He writes, "The principal characteristic of Third Cinema is really not so much where it is made, or even who makes it, but, rather, the ideology it espouses and the consciousness it displays."[46] Third Cinema is a weapon for independent filmmakers in both the East and the West to wrest representational control away from dominant European and American cinema. Second, Gabriel is not rallying for a politics of association that his Western critics desire because he is calling for a politics of affiliation. The latter arranges resistance against global imperialism not in terms of identity but rather in terms of structural logic. In other words, it successfully frees politics of opposition to global capitalism from the narrow confines of national borders to claim that the current directions of European and American imperial politics affect people in the global South as it does those in metropolitan New York or downtown Seattle.

Willemen only appears to speak for the Third World's rights. His actual intention is to rephrase intellectually the narrative of the West as the only universal versus the East as particularly marked. However, unlike its use in the previous centuries, in the late twentieth century this discourse is couched in rhetoric that makes it appear as speaking in support of the Other. That said, we should not unconditionally dismiss Willemen's essay. His critique of Gabriel does have a few useful points to offer. Indeed, Gabriel's internationalist vision can be held guilty of homogenizing existing particularities, tensions, and inequalities within Third World nation states, thereby re-creating an image of the Third World far distant from the reality of the Third Worlds. For, as Willemen notes, issues of ethnicity and gender (and class) appear absent from Gabriel's conception of Third

World cinema. Similarly, Third World directors such as Ritwik Ghatak, whose films resist myopic nationalism as well as teary-eyed cosmopolitanism, have no position in Gabriel's writings. Like Willemen, Ranjana Khanna also notes Third Cinema's failure to address gender politics within the Third World and Third World films. Besides, Gabriel's emphasis on revolutionary man-making implicates Third Cinema, like its adversary First and Second Cinemas, in the process of subject-production. In promoting the idea of fashioning man through the fires of socialist revolutions, Gabriel's Third Cinema reprises the essentialist Eurocentric (and Christological) fantasy of Man as a subject of History (and historical redemption).

Nonetheless, Third Cinema provides an invaluable point of departure for thinking about postcolonial film theory. Its fundamental thrust is political, and it aims at constructing a political vision that responds to the exigencies that global capitalism and the new imperialism foist on the planet. It is not simply a mode of resistance but also a promotion of destabilizing as a mode of political being, even for those within the First World. It is not defined by geographical space but by the position that one advocates and the identity that one adopts. Postcolonial film theory should operate in the same manner as Third Cinema—expansive and yet constantly dismantling even its own emergent hierarchies.

Toward a postcolonial film theory

Robert Stam rightly argues that Third Cinema in the present has multiplied and branched into "accented," "exilic," "diasporic," "transnational," and "intercultural" cinemas.[47] Instead of one group or style of cinema dealing with culture and ethnic, gender, and political identities of peoples from different parts of the globe, we now have many in tune with the globalization of cultures and associated identities. These differently labeled cinemas constitute the nontraditional narrative communities of this century. They tell particularistic rather than universal stories and feature characters with "multiple, hybridized, crossed, and performative identities" that struggle to assimilate in a new country amid the loss of "imagined" homelands.[48] As such the spirit of Third Cinema courses through these films as they act as the repository for absence constituted by the marginalized.

But does the emergence of accented, exilic, diasporic, transnational cinemas imply an end to the Third Cinema's political project of dismantling realities composed by dominant cinema? Do the growth in number of non-Western films screened in the West and an increased presence of non-Western filmmakers and actors in Hollywood make the Third Cinema ideology obsolete? This is similar to the question postcolonial theorists ask in the context of teaching postcolonial cinema in American universities. While teaching other cultures seems necessary in a rapidly globalizing world, the fact that the idea of multiculturalism makes people feel good guides much of what universities teach. While almost every American university has courses devoted to postcolonial literature and film, often these courses exist as token representations of the Other rather than being functionally integrated into the curricula to allow students to develop an understanding of cinema as part of a world system of signs. In order to escape tokenism when viewing postcolonial films, a basis in postcolonial film theory is requisite. While postcolonial theory has been praised for the current internationalization of Western humanities curricula, the function of postcolonial theory has not come to an end with the spread of non-Western literature or film courses in the academy. To the contrary, the need to rigorously revive the discipline has increased.

Likewise, formulating a postcolonial theory of film is also needed. A reimagined postcolonial theory needs to be routed through the principles of the Third Cinema movement if a theory for postcolonial analysis of cinema is to be properly worked out. At a time when Hollywood's cultural and political sensitivity toward the Other has complicated the job of examining the processes via which legitimizations of the West's hegemony continue to unfold, I wish to take cue from Third Cinema's emphasis on unveiling Hollywood's construction of onscreen realities and audiences as subjects desirous of those realities. Films do not simply show what objects to desire but it also teaches audiences how to desire, and this is what the postcolonial film theorist must analyze.

The fundamental challenge for postcolonial film theory today lies in unraveling Eurocentrism that circulates under the guise of progressive discourses in current Hollywood cinema. It needs to render visible the tangible and intangible ideological processes via which Hollywood constitutes a neocolonial aesthetic, and the social, political, and psychic realities of the present. As such, postcolonial film theory should examine the manufacture and dissemination of knowledge in dominant cinema; inquire into the end results of such manufacture, including dissemination patterns and circulation logic; and, finally, unmask the rhetorical processes of subject-production ideologically cloaked through culturally sensitive representations of the non-west.

In their 1983 essay "Colonialism, Race, and Representation," co-authors Robert Stam and Louise Spence discuss the need to look beyond surface-level representation in cinema and understand the ideological function of films as producing desirable realities.[49] They begin by characterizing the existing "studies of filmic colonialism and racism" as "marred" by "methodological naiveté" (an assessment valid even today). They write:

> While posing legitimate questions concerning narrative plausibility and mimetic accuracy, negative stereotypes and positive images, the emphasis on realism has often betrayed an exaggerated faith in the possibilities of verisimilitude in art in general and the cinema in particular, avoiding the fact that films are inevitably constructs, fabrications, representations.[50]

They charge most critical analyses of cinema with resembling literary analyses, lacking any engagement with "specifically cinematic dimensions." Drawing out the difference between cinema as representation and cinema as re-presentation, that is between cinema as embodied authentic speech and cinema as indirect, reported, or proxy speech, the authors argue for shifting focus to the cinematic apparatus, the symbolic codes of cinema, and not just on what is shown but what is not shown. Silences, absences, and misdirection in the filmic narrative are equally ideological. They urge accordingly for critically intervening to show how these absences and misdirections deviate audience attention from the real conditions in the outside world. The issue is not whether a film correctly represents reality but what it constructs as the reality.

Postcolonial film theory should study "how consciousness and systems of value are created [in cinema to] either bind society or illuminate its fissures."[51] A postcolonial theory of film should be able to historicize cinematic manufacture of reality by identifying visible and invisible structures of oppression, hegemony, and Othering in relation to past and continuing forms of European imperialisms. None of these mean that examinations of representation and misrepresentation of the Other must be forsaken. Rather a postcolonial analysis should be also able to explicate the particular or general consciousness crafted through a film narrative that is responsible for abject representations of the Other contrasted to images of Western plenitude passing unregistered.

Postcolonial film theory must function actively to unravel latent structures of Eurocentrism through interrogations of structural inconsistencies in discourse and cinematic textualizations of the colony, postcolony, and the native Other. It should employ strategies of forced readings so as to uplift the veil covering Eurocentric representations of an exclusive European modernity. Forced reading as a performance of scrupulous travesty, to use Spivak's phrase, when pursued to expunge narratives of their ingrained European privilege, can produce a counternarrative for making visible the absence of a subject whose lack makes possible Europe's position as the subject of discourse.

In the chapter that follows, I take up some of these theoretical avenues to read James Cameron's *Avatar* as a characteristic example of contemporary discourse. Its manifest critique of global imperialism hides its scrupulous reinvention of a Western subjectivity at the expense of the indigenous Na'vi. My analysis focuses on reading this concealed narrative of subject formation and the concurrent silencing of the Na'vi to further elaborate the connection between contemporary discourses critical of imperialism and neocolonialism and the systemic production of knowledge. I will amplify how colonial ideas—images, themes, categories of definition pertaining to the lexicalization of the native to the Western self as a self-consolidating Other—continue to circulate in Cameron's film in the guise of political correctness, ecological sensitivity, and multicultural globalization.

Notes

1 Stuart Hall, "When was 'The Postcolonial'? Thinking at the Limit," in *The Post-Colonial Question: Common Skies, Divided Horizons*, eds Iain Chambers and Lidia Curti (London: Routledge, 1996), 250.

2 Slavoj Žižek, "A Plea for Leninist Intolerance," *Critical Inquiry* 28.2 (2002): 545.

3 See, for instance, William David Hart, "Slavoj Žižek and the Imperial/Colonial Model of Religion," *Nepantla: Views from South* 3.3 (2002): 553–578; and Gautam Basu Thakur, "The Menon-Žižek Debate: The Tale of the (Never-marked) (But secretly coded) Universal and the (Always marked) Particular . . .," *Slavic Review* 72.4 (2013): 750–770.

4 Aijaz Ahmad, *In Theory: Nations, Classes, Literatures* (London: Verso, 2008), 7.

5 Like Ahmad, Masao Miyoshi identifies the rise of postcolonial theory among Western academics as a way of avoiding the analysis of the actual contemporary political situation. Politics proper remains mostly unaddressed in postcolonial analyses.

Globalization, for Miyoshi, is nothing but a deepening of the colonialist impulse, which is why he calls for the reinvention of postcolonial theory as "a rigorous political and economic scrutiny rather than a gesture of pedagogic expediency." Masao Miyoshi, "A Borderless World? From Colonialism to Transnationalism and the Decline of the Nation-State," *Critical Inquiry* 19.4 (1993): 751.

6 See Abdul JanMohamed, "The Economy of Manichean Allegory: The Function of Racial Difference in Colonialist Literature," in *"Race," Writing, and Difference*, ed. Henry Louis Gates, Jr. (Chicago/London: University of Chicago Press, 1986), 78–105; and Arif Dirlik, *The Postcolonial Aura: Third World Criticism in the Age of Global Capitalism* (Boulder, CO: Westview Press, 1997).

7 See Benita Parry, *Postcolonial Studies: A Materialist Critique* (London: Routledge, 2004); Benita Parry and Laura Chrisman, "Editor's Introduction," in *Essays and Studies: Postcolonial Theory and Criticism* 52 (1999): vii–xi; and Benita Parry, "Problems in Current Theories of Colonial Discourse," in *The Post-colonial Studies Reader*, eds Bill Ashcroft, Gareth Griffiths, and Helen Tiffin (London: Routledge, 1995), 36–44.

8 See Partha Chatterjee, *Nation and its Fragments: Colonial and Postcolonial Histories* (Princeton: Princeton University Press, 1993); and Chinua Achebe, "Foreword," in *Igbo Arts: Community and Cosmos*, eds H. M. Cole and C. C. Aniakor (Los Angeles: Museum of Cultural History, UCLA, 1984), ix.

9 Bankim Chandra Chatterjee, *Bankim Rochanabali* [The Collected Works of Bankim Chandra Chatterjee], vol. 2 (Calcutta: Dey's Publishing, 2007), 330–333; 336–340.

10 Gayatri Chakravorty Spivak, "Three Women's Texts and a Critique of Imperialism," *Critical Inquiry* 12.1 (1985): 235–236.

11 Edward Said, *Orientalism* (New York: Vintage, 1979), 6.

12 My argument in this paragraph consciously parallels Slavoj Žižek's criticism of culture studies and Todd McGowan's criticism of film studies. I believe all three disciplines—culture studies, film studies, and postcolonial studies—ail from a similar problem. They are not theoretical enough. In context of the culture studies, Žižek reminds us that it is the reticence to embrace more radical aspects of Marxist thought—culture studies' preference for a

sanitized Marx over a radically political Lenin—which is responsible for the dearth of any new radical research in the field. McGowan raises a similar red flag in context of film studies when he claims that film studies is not Lacanian enough. It is interesting to note that in the cases of both postcolonial and film studies, Freudian-Lacanian thought was singled out for special treatment. If Parry and others sought to completely excise the use of Lacan from postcolonial theory, David Bordwell did the same for film studies. Given that this book engages postcolonially with film, it might prove to be an opportunity for reclaiming the position of psychoanalytic thought in both disciplines.

13 Frantz Fanon, *Black Skin, White Masks*, trans. Charles Lamm Markmann (New York: Grove Weidenfield, 1967), 18.

14 Fanon, *Black Skin*, 112–113.

15 Fanon, *Black Skins*, 11.

16 Frantz Fanon, *The Wretched of the Earth*, trans. Richard Philcox (New York: Grove Press, 2004), 2.

17 Homi Bhabha, "Framing Fanon," Foreword to Frantz Fanon, *The Wretched of the Earth*, trans. Richard Philcox (New York: Grove Press, 2004), ix–x.

18 East has always been a fungible category for the West. If to England, France, and other Western European colonial powers, the East primarily meant Middle East, South and Southeast Asia, after the Second World War and emergence of the United States as an imperial power, the imaginary shifted more toward South East and the Pacific. Even though it is not to the east of Europe but south, European discourses would often describe Africa with some of the same stereotypes used to describe South Asia and its inhabitants.

19 Said, *Orientalism*, 63.

20 Homi Bhabha, "Signs Taken for Wonders," in *The Location of Culture* (London: Routledge, 1994), 153.

21 Homi Bhabha, "The Other Question," in *The Location of Culture* (London: Routledge, 1994), 94–95.

22 Homi Bhabha, "How Newness Enters the World," in *The Location of Culture* (London: Routledge, 1994), 322.

23 For a fuller elaboration of this position on Bhabha, see Gautam Basu Thakur, "Reading Bhabha, Reading Lacan: Preliminary

Notes on Colonial Anxiety," in *The Literary Lacan from Literature to "lituraterre" and Beyond*, ed. Santanu Biswas (London: Seagull Books, 2013).

24 These lines are freely borrowed from Derrida's *Specters of Marx* (and mediated through Lacan) to summarize how the vernacular nonsense or unreadable other hauntingly deconstructs the imperial cartography of knowledge. See Jacques Derrida, *Specters of Marx: The State of Debt, the Work of Mourning, and the New International*, trans. Peggy Kamuf (London: Routledge, 1994), 6; and Serge Cottet, *Freud and the Desire of the Psychoanalyst* (London: Karnac Books, 2012), 10.

25 Gayatri Spivak and Sarah Harasym, *The Post-Colonial Critic: Interviews, Strategies, Dialogues* (New York: Routledge, 1990).

26 Gayatri Chakravorty Spivak, "Can the Subaltern Speak?," in *Marxism and the Interpretation of Culture*, eds Cary Nelson and Lawrence Grossberg (Urbana: University of Illinois Press, 1988), 271–313.

27 Gayatri Chakravorty Spivak, in Leon de Kock, "Interview With Gayatri Chakravorty Spivak: New Nation Writers Conference in South Africa," *Ariel: A Review of International English Literature* 23.3 (1992): 45–46.

28 Gayatri Chakravorty Spivak, "Scattered Speculations on the Subaltern and the Popular," *Postcolonial Studies* 8.4 (2005): 477.

29 Gayatri Chakravorty Spivak, *In Other Worlds: Essays in Cultural Politics* (New York: Routledge, 1998), 281.

30 Veena Das, "Subaltern as Perspective," in *Subaltern Studies* 6 (New Delhi: Oxford University Press, 1989), 310.

31 See Jacques Derrida, *The Animal That Therefore I Am*, trans. David Wills, ed. Marie-Louise Mallet (New York: Fordham University Press, 2008).

32 Susan Hayward, "Postcolonial Theory," in *Cinema Studies: The Key Concepts* (Hoboken: Taylor and Francis, 2012), 283.

33 Robert Stam, *Film Theory: An Introduction* (Malden: Wiley Blackwell, 2000), 102.

34 Hayward, "Postcolonial Theory," 283.

35 See Sandra Ponzanesi and Marguerite Waller, eds, *Postcolonial Cinema Studies* (Hoboken: Taylor and Francis, 2011); Elizabeth

Heffelfinge and Laura Wright, *Visual Difference: Postcolonial Studies and Intercultural Cinema* (New York: Peter Lang, 2011); and Rebecca Weaver-Hightower and Peter Hulme, *Postcolonial Film: History, Empire, Resistance* (Hoboken: Taylor and Francis, 2014).

36 See Fernando Solanas and Octavio Getino, "Towards a Third Cinema" in *New Latin American Cinema*, vol. 1, ed. Michael T. Martin (Detroit: Wayne State University Press, 1997), 35.

37 See Teshome H. Gabriel, "Towards a Critical Theory of Third World Films," in *Colonial Discourse and Postcolonial Theory*, eds Patrick Williams and Laura Chrisman (New York: Columbia University Press, 1994), 340–358. For Gabriel's discussion of specific features of Third Cinema including its activist and extra-cinematic aesthetics, as well as its emphasis on critical spectatorship, see Teshome H. Gabriel, "Third Cinema as Guardian of Popular Memory: Towards a Third Aesthetics," in *Questions of Third Cinema*, eds Jim Pines and Paul Willemen (London: BFI Publishing, 1989), 57–61.

38 Teshome Gabriel, "Third Cinema Updated: Exploration of Nomadic Aesthetics & Narrative Communities," *Teshome Gabriel: Articles and Other Works*, http://teshomegabriel.net/third-cinema-updated.

39 Gabriel, "Third Cinema Updated," http://teshomegabriel.net/third-cinema-updated.

40 Solanas and Getino, *Third Cinema*, 42–43.

41 Gabriel, "Towards," 347–348.

42 For an example, see Gabriel's essay on Ousmane Sembène's *Xala*. Teshome Gabriel, "Xala: A Cinema of Wax and Gold," in *Jump Cut: Hollywood, Politics, and Counter Cinema*, ed. Peter Steven (New York: Praeger, 1985): 334–343.

43 See Paul Willemen, "The Third Cinema Question: Notes and Reflections," in *Questions of Third Cinema*, eds Jim Pines and Paul Willemen (London: BFI Publishing, 1989), 221–251.

44 Critics like Ismail Xavier and Robert Stam also contend that there is a direct connection between nationalism and Third Cinema.

45 Stam, *Film Theory*, 102.

46 Gabriel, "Third Cinema as Guardian of Popular Memory," 55.

47 Stam, *Film Theory*, 292.

48 Hamid Naficy, *An Accented Cinema: Exilic and Diasporic Filmmaking* (Princeton: Princeton University Press, 2001), 269.

49 See Robert Stam and Louise Spence, "Colonialism, Race, and Representation," *Screen* 24.2 (1983), 2–20.

50 Stam and Spence, "Colonialism," 3.

51 Toby Miller, "Introduction," in *A Companion to Film Theory*, eds Toby Miller and Robert Stam (Oxford: Blackwell, 1999), 4.

CHAPTER TWO

Postcolonial Theory and *Avatar*, Or, Postcolonial Criticism in a Multicultural World

Imagining other worlds?

Avatar ranks in *Time* magazine's list of the top 100 films of all time. There it rubs shoulders with Michelangelo Antonioni's *Blow-Up* (1966) and Satyajit Ray's *Apu Trilogy* (1955–1959). It is also the highest grossing film of all time. What accounts for its unprecedented critical and box-office success? What places James Cameron next to auteurs like Ray and Antonioni? If for the moment we suspend the usual argument about the film's use of cutting edge digital technology, then the answer becomes quite difficult to provide. Popular opinion about *Avatar* is split down the middle, and this represents a problem of reading and interpretation. To some, Cameron's film is a masterpiece—a bold critique of the West's colonial histories and its current involvement in neocolonial resource wars, a metaphorical commentary about our fascination with materialism and its effects on ecology, and a chastising reminder of globalization's mishandling of indigenous populations throughout the world. To others, *Avatar* is a clichéd repetition of the white messiah narrative—a racist and conservative account of a white hero saving a native population in civilizational crisis and marrying the tribal princess to become the chief of the tribe. Hollywood has spun these narratives consistently over the years, as attested to by films such as *Dune* (1984), *Dances With Wolves* (1990), and *Pocahontas* (1995).[1]

This debate fundamentally misses the point. In fact, the debate over reading *Avatar* is itself ideological insofar as it performs the very excision that ideology always demands. That is to say, as each side performs its reading of the film on the basis of what is visually or thematically represented in the cinematic narrative, they foreclose through the cultural production of meaning the subtle politics of subject formation in the text. A critical analysis of *Avatar* must extend beyond the representational to address the discursive reimagination of Western subjectivity in the film. Viewing Cameron's film through the postcolonial lens, this chapter will analyze the mechanism of subject-production in the film.

Colonial discourse has always been involved in finding tangible and intangible ways to constitute the subject of the West in difference from the non-Western Other. Though colonialism came to an ostensible end in the mid-twentieth century, it left behind the discursive mechanisms for facilitating the continuous reproduction of sovereign Western subjectivity. Subject-production continued through the late twentieth century and now in the twenty-first century, though it has undergone certain changes in recent years in response to neoliberal ideologies of globalization. My analysis here will highlight some of the ways in which subject-production unfolds in *Avatar*, which is a fundamental concern of postcolonial theory insofar as Western subject-production occurs through the constitution of the non-Western Other.

The subject of the West in *Avatar* is a reimagined subject. This reimagination has been rendered necessary by the radically altered geopolitical climate of the twenty-first century. On the one hand, the West's involvement in the war in the

Middle East, its aggressive foreign and economic policies, and its systematized practices of racial and class apartheid within its national borders have created a negative image in the eyes of the global public. On the other hand, increasing demands within Western communities for multiculturalism and growing concerns over ecology and race relations have made "change" a governing word in the discourse of social reform. *Avatar* responds to both these vectors by redrawing the Western subject at a distance from the negative images of corporate militarism and in tune with the liberal beliefs of the twenty-first century. Put differently, *Avatar* revises the image of the West from a racist, imperialist, political bully to that of a multicultural, tolerant, racially and ecologically sensitive subject. It carves this alternate iconography through the figure of Jake Sully (Sam Worthington), whose subjectivity is constituted through the film narrative.

The anti-imperialist narrative of *Avatar* obscures a deeply Eurocentric mindset. In the guise of criticizing the West's violent appropriations of the Other, the film actually rehearses the old colonial narratives of European privilege, entitlement, and sovereign subjectivity. Even Sully's subject formation is carried out through symbols, metaphors, and, to use Spivak's words, acts of "soul-making" that are deeply reminiscent of subject-production in colonial discourses. Yet all these are hidden from plain sight through a narrative that critiques colonial and neocolonial expansionism and privileges the indigene other.

Sully is the avatar of the West in the global present. His figure is constructed, first, by contrasting him to the corporate-militarism of RDA (Resources Development Administration) and, then, by differentiating him from the indigenous Na'vi. An instrument of Enlightenment reason, Sully's subjectivity is underwritten by a mishmash of nineteenth-century colonial discourse and a healthy dose of twenty-first-century liberal attitudes. On the one hand, he is marked by moral uprightness, sincerity of labor, and respect for the Other, and, on the other hand, he is the poster child of the liberal enterprise who retains possession of the means to politicize the destiny of the oppressed.

In what follows, I bring to light the rhetoric mechanisms through which European dominance over the native other is reimagined and reclaimed through the figure of Sully. My investigation however will not be limited to reading the cinematic narrative only. I will bring alongside my discussion of the film select scholarly writings on the film in order to examine how these academic discourses unwittingly participate in and consolidate the cultural production of meaning attempted in the film. The essays I consider—Todd McGowan's "Maternity Divided: *Avatar* and the Enjoyment of Nature" (2010), Dana Fore's "The Tracks of Sully's Tears: Disability in James Cameron's *Avatar*" (2011), and, Adam Davis's "Native Images: The Otherness and Affectivity of the Digital Body" (2013)—read Cameron's film as an alternative commentary on contemporary filmmaking as well as global politics. They focus on Cameron's use of unreadable bodies (photographic, animated, disabled) and politicization of Nature to explore the ideological character of the film text.[2] While structurally analogous to the postcolonial methodology of identifying the marginal as constitutive of the hegemonic, these essays nonetheless suffer because of their lack of engagement with the postcolonial question. The analyses are not necessarily incorrect, but by overlooking the issue of subject-production in the film, these essays underwrite instead of challenge the hegemonic dispensations of Cameron's film. This also compromises the potential of these essays to adequately unravel the myriad workings of ideology in the global present, rendering them in the process unsuspecting compradors in Hollywood's cultural production of meaning at the expense of the Other. As such, when taken together and read in adjacency, the cinematic imaginary and the university discourse reveal their respective yet mutual Eurocentric biases.

In the mid-1980s, Gayatri Spivak drew attention to the underlying presence of Eurocentrism in habitual as well as radical conversations emerging out of the West. She had shown radical philosophical inquiries casually overwriting the Third-World-gendered subaltern by appropriating her within axiomatic structures of European hetero-patriarchy. Today, after almost three decades, and the postcolonial and posthumanist revolutions in the academy later, there is still no sign of an end to this. Eurocentrism continues to circulate through discourses of the West in various forms and in countless disguises. Cameron's *Avatar* is just a recent example. This chapter constitutes yet another effort to identify, analyze, and deconstruct this longstanding narrative of Europe as the universal and the Other as particular. Taking my cue from Spivak's incisive critique of Deleuze's and Foucault's conflation of the aesthetic notion of re-presentation (*darstellen*) with political representation or representation as "speaking for" (*vertreten*), I want to charge Cameron's cinematic discourse for performing the same excision in *Avatar* by using some of the same means employed by the celebrated European philosophers in their discussion of Third World labor. I will show that far from advocating the cause of the Third World indigene, which the film claims to do and which Cameron has claimed in innumerous interviews as his original intention in making the film, *Avatar* reassigns the Other under the signature of Europe. Cameron's brand of Hollywood Marxism describes the contemporary "scene of power" in order to rearrange the privileged subjectivity of the West through representation of "an essentialist, utopian politics."[3]

Avatar produces a normative, self-reflexive, Western subjectivity through effacements of native cultures, politics, society, and desire. Though its plot appears to do just the opposite—that is, galvanize opinion against violence perpetrated against indigenous populations of the globe—the film is rife with recognizable and clandestine acts of violent othering of the Other. These begin with the representation of the Na'vi as differently colored, nonhuman noble savages to depictions of the Na'vi as lacking complex social structures to representations of the Na'vi as incapable of historicizing their political destiny without external (that is, European) aid. My reading of the film will focus on a set of moments or scenes to delineate the subject-production of Sully through acts of othering the Na'vi. I will discuss how the film inconspicuously constitutes Sully's subjectivity by playing on the current cultural fantasy of making society into an organic whole by reconnecting with nature and establishing racial, cultural, and interspecies solidarity. Sully figures in this schema as the subject stewarding this idea into a reality.

Before moving ahead, I should clarify that I will not examine the film in sequence. That is to say, the scenes as I analyze them do not strictly refer to a temporally bound sequence of events from the film. My reason for doing this is to emphasize how atemporal events and events that are absent in the narrative can be inferred in logical consequence to what is present. In other words, I rearrange the chronological in order to unstitch the foreclosed meanings of a hidden narrative of subject-production.

Scene I: the emptiness of Pandora (representation)

Imperial representations of the colony are always underwritten by the fantasy of the empty land. This fantasy serves the purpose of legitimizing territorial conquests and settlement of lands deemed uninhabited. The material script of this fantasy or its juridical embodiment was known as the principle of *terra nullius*. It metaphorically populated the empty, unsubstantiated fantasy of the virgin Other land through the "Biblical idea of creation *ex nihilo*," on the one hand, and "Locke's idea of the *tabula rasa*," on the other, to compose a comfortable and reliable "unity of imperial politics, theology, and epistemology."[4] The discourse formed thus dictates the free use of Western (in this case of English) law on lands considered lawless and uninhabited. "Uninhabited" in most cases implies that the English considered the indigenous populations of the land

FIGURE 1 *The empty land (*Avatar*, 2009)*

nonhuman or inferior to the English, therefore automatically excluded from the English law. European occupations in Africa, Asia, and Australia notoriously used the principle of *terra nullius* throughout the colonial period for their legitimization. It also plays a part in other imperial contexts such as in the discourses of manifest destiny in North America and the rhetoric of the Nazi "East" in Europe.[5]

One of the earliest uses of the empty land rhetoric is found in Homer's *Odyssey*. In book IX, Homer uses it to describe the land of the Cyclops and to justify Odysseus's representation of the natives as monster. Odysseus narrates his first glimpse of the land of the Cyclops (and he gathers all this information even before setting foot on the land) to the Phoenician king Alkinoos in the following manner:

> In the next land we found the Kyklopes,
> giants, louts, without a law to bless them.
> In ignorance leaving the fruitage of the earth in mystery
> to the immortal gods, they neither plow
> nor sow by hand, nor till the ground, though grain –
> wild wheat and barley – grows untended, and

> wine-grapes, in clusters, ripen in heaven's rain.
> Kyklopes have no muster and no meeting,
> no consultation or old tribal ways,
> but each one dwells in his own mountain cave
> dealing out rough justice to wife and child,
> indifferent to what the others do.[6]

The dehumanization of the Cyclops in these lines has a parallel in Odysseus's deep regret over the untapped natural resources of the land—resources that the Cyclops themselves are too lazy and too unsophisticated to exploit. This gesture of devaluing native enterprise (the Cyclops are hunter-gatherers bereft of agriculture, consequently lacking in civic values) empties the fertile land in preparation for the landing party. This is the primary ideological purpose of this fantasy—the land is untended and its weaker inhabitants (women and children) are oppressed, therefore it is the duty of the West to interfere into and intervene for the preservation of a universally valid moral law alongside taking the responsibility of tillage (or, colonial labor) on the side.

What stands out here is the rhetorical connection between Homer's poem and the modern-day colonial representations of the savage Other in their virgin lands. Given the similarities between these it is not a stretch of the imagination to say that Homer's epic establishes the protocols for describing the Other that finds itself repeated in real and fictional representations of the colonized. For example, one sees the repurposing of the empty land fantasy in classics of the English canon all the way from William Shakespeare's *Tempest* (1610), John Donne's "Elegy to his Mistress Going to Bed" (1654), and Daniel Defoe's *Robinson Crusoe* (1719) to William Cowper's "The Solitude of Alexander Selkirk" (1782), Rudyard Kipling's "The Man Who Would be King" (1888), and William Golding's *Lord of the Flies* (1954). More recently, the same dynamic appears in Hollywood films such as Peter Weir's *The Mosquito Coast* (1986), Robert Zemeckis's *Cast Away* (2000), and Cameron's *Avatar*.

But this is neither a matter of recycling a fictional trope nor an issue of citation. Consider for instance the following passage from Charles Darwin's *The Descent of Man* (1871). In this Darwin is writing about his experience of first seeing the natives of the island Tierra del Fuego:

> The astonishment which I felt on first seeing a party of Fuegians on a wild and broken shore will never be forgotten by me. . . . These men were absolutely naked and bedaubed with paint, their long hair was tangled, their mouths frothed with excitement, and their expressions were wild, startled, and distrustful. They possessed hardly any arts, and like wild animals lived on what they could catch; they had no government, and were merciless to everyone not of their own small tribe . . . a savage who delights to torture his enemies, offers up bloody sacrifices, practices infanticide without remorse, treats his wives like slaves, knows no decency, and is haunted by the grossest superstitions.[7]

The similarities between Darwin's description of the Fuegians and Homer's description of the Cyclops are too striking to be missed.

Darwin is not citing Homer consciously, but the celebrated scientist's almost verbatim reproduction of Homeric metaphors for describing the Fuegians is a product of that organized body of thinking about the non-West which Said terms Orientalism. The matter of citation in Darwin is unconscious—not unconscious in the sense of unknown but unconscious in the form of repetition. What repeats through the thousands of years separating Homer from Darwin, and then unfolds beyond Darwin into our present, is the fantastic image of otherness as dispossession. It is the phantasmic screen that pivots the West's material interests and spiritual investments in the East. The Other imagined naked is the Other under a mark of negation. The Other land as vacant, the Other as impoverished, the Other as helpless or violent conveniently underwrite the West's exercises of territorial as well as imaginative conquests of the Other alongside symbolically constituting an identity for the West in difference to the Other. In *Avatar* we see the same logical fantasy at work.

Pandora and the politicization of emptiness

Avatar's cinematic universe and mythography evokes a profound sense of emptiness through its act of naming or signification, especially its use of the names "Pandora" and "Polyphemus." Polyphemus is a giant gas planet orbiting the star Alpha Centauri A and Pandora is the largest moon orbiting the planet Polyphemus.[8] Both names summon images of emptiness. Pandora reminds us of the Greek myth about hope as the only thing remaining in the world after Pandora opens the box out of curiosity. Polyphemus is the name of the one-eyed "monster" in Homer's epic whom Odysseus defeats. But these names do something more than just allude to earlier texts. They condition audiences to view the images on screen by calling into memory the specific signifieds attached strictly to the signifiers "Pandora" and "Polyphemus." The notion of emptiness is phonetically glued to these two unique proper names. It can be recognized by most audiences in metropolitan centers of the globe, thanks again to colonialism that controlled over 80 percent of the world and introduced Western education into most of these regions. The names synchronize the film in relation to the imperial imaginary of the empty land, territorial conquests of these lands, and a corresponding suspicion of women and the racial Other as irresponsible.[9]

The purported emptiness of Pandora is crucial for the subject-production of Sully. Beginning with his insertion into the military unit on the planet to his becoming a member of the Omaticaya tribe, emptiness is diversely used and referenced in the film narrative to prop Sully's subjectivity. Sully describes himself as "empty" at the very start of the film complaining about a "void" or "hole" in his life. Later, he describes himself again as an "empty cup" when speaking to the Omaticaya shaman Mo'at (CCH Pounder). We also hear the lead scientist Dr. Grace Augustine (Sigourney Weaver) mock Sully by calling him a "jarhead." But apart from these references, emptiness structures and arranges the narrative of Sully's subject formation in two distinct ways: first, by giving symbolic value to Sully's individualistic enterprise; and second, by metaphorically presenting the Na'vi as lacking the capacity to politicize their destiny without the help of Sully. Both these rearrange Sully from a dispossessed, disabled veteran to that of singular universal in authorial charge of the "wretched of the earth."

The formation of Sully's subjectivity is not dependent simply on presenting him as empathic with and respectful of the indigenous other. Besides Sully, Grace and Norm Spellman (Joel David Moore) are sympathetic to the Na'vi cause as well. They are studiously respectful of Pandora and the Na'vi way of life. Yet what differentiates Sully from them is his individualistic approach to whatever life throws his way and his ability to conjoin two extremely significant imperial signatures—his participation as a liberty-loving subject in the discourse of enterprise and his entrepreneurial labor. The implicit premise of the empty land and its incapable (or lacking) natives determine fully the symbolic superiority of Sully's subjectivity.

The enterprise of Sully

Reena Dube explains the discourse of enterprise as one of the means by which colonial hegemony establishes itself over the colonized. Emerging out of post-Enlightenment ideas, the primary aim of this discourse is to control the production of knowledge within the colony and represent colonialism as necessary labor. In particular, the discourse was used to devalue native labor and to stress the value of the colonizer's entrepreneurial labor in order to mark it as the guarantee of the colonizer's right over the Other's land. It attributes the success of colonialism to European individualism and the strength of European character, ignoring the exploitation of cheap native labor as well as military and economic force used to extract that labor. The colonizer's untiring industry against the most "inhospitable material conditions of production" was presented as the ultimate proof of European authority over the colony.[10]

Cameron's film presents the discourse of enterprise in another way. It redraws the binary arrangement between the entrepreneurial colonizer and the abject colonized. Though the colonized or Na'vi stay in their designated position as abject and dispossessed, it is the position of the colonizer that is intelligently tweaked in the film for the recomposition of Sully's subjectivity in contrast to both the RDA and the Na'vi.[11] Though in the position of the colonizer, the military-corporation appears incapable of any productive enterprise of labor primarily due to its failure to conjoin their labor to a discourse of liberal humanism. The RDA fully subscribes to the discourse of enterprise: they devalue indigenous labor and regret the inadequate use of the inexhaustible natural resources of the land by the Na'vi. However, the RDA fails in responsible stewardship of the land's resources and its people. It fails to promote itself as a liberty-loving, liberty-guaranteeing, and liberty-securing institution. Dube reminds us that this façade of liberalism was integral to the colonial discourse of enterprise as the iconic English entrepreneur was imagined as successfully earning profit without appearing to curtail the liberties of the Other. When audiences enter Pandora along with Sully, the RDA is already prepared to shed its liberal mask after years of frustration caused by the reluctance of the Na'vi to cooperate with their mining operations. Both Colonel Miles Quaritch (Stephen Lang) and Parker Selfridge (Giovanni Ribisi), RDA's head of security and head of corporate affairs respectively, make their positions unambiguously clear: they are on Pandora for profit. While "killing the indigenous looks bad," it becomes unavoidable with quarterly balance statements at stake. With liberty so openly dismissed for profit, the reimagination of

Sully becomes imperative. And in the course of the film, Sully's love for liberty alongside his entrepreneurial labor contrast his subjectivity against the ruthless profiteering character of the RDA.

Unlike the belligerent and caricaturized agents of the RDA, Sully appears from the very beginning of the film as independent, and though derided by many for being a jarhead, in possesion of an active mind. The composed tone of his voice, first heard as a voiceover, and his self-respecting attitude, reflected in his refusals of aid from anyone wishing to help him because of his paraplegic condition, establish Sully in the initial shots of the film as different from most humans on Pandora. Though we see him agreeing to work as Quaritch's plant in the science team, he does not come across as a lackey. He appears more like someone who listens to his heart. It is, however, only after meeting the Na'vi and learning their way of life that Sully's character achieves its full potential. We witness his gradual transformation from being an informant for the company to becoming a liberator of the oppressed.

Sully does not gain entry into the Omaticaya tribe easily. The failure of previous missions to diplomatically engage with the Na'vi and the RDA's continuing operations in Pandora make his acceptance doubly difficult. Yet Sully is able to convince Mo'at that he truly wants to learn from the Na'vi. Mo'at consequently makes Sully's entry into the Omaticaya clan dependent on him learning the Na'vi way of life. And Sully works hard to eventually earn his place as one of the tribe. The film shows his labor extensively—from his patient exercises trying to ride the Direhorse to him learning about the local customs, and, finally, establishing a bond with a Banshee. It is only after he successfully finishes his lessons and forges a respectful relationship with the land, its animals, and Na'vi culture through his non-violent and non-exploitative labor that he becomes initiated into the clan. A futuristic Robinson Crusoe, Sully establishes a connection with Pandora through respectful labor, thereby replacing the RDA in the neocolonial universe of the film with his rational, freedom-loving, culturally sensitive, and labor-intensive self.

But what about the Na'vi? If the discourse of enterprise involves the complementary devaluation of native labor and culture, then the film appears to do the opposite with regard to the Na'vi. Cameron presents Na'vi society as highly idealized and not at all devalued in the film. But in order to get the entire picture, it is imperative to view Sully's subject-production in the context of his gradual rise within the hierarchy of Na'vi society, a rise that ends with his emergence as the unquestioned leader of the tribe. His social rise is only made possible by contrasting his character to that of the Na'vi. The singular lack in the Na'vi is their incapability to organize themselves into a political group. The Na'vi cannot politicize their destiny. Sully fulfills this lack, uniting the Na'vi against the oppressive RDA.

The Na'vi serve the function of a backdrop to Sully's pursuit of labor, liberty, and individualism. Their oppressed and marginal position makes possible Sully's role as the savior of the oppressed. He is responsible for representing the Na'vi, for making their voices heard and their speech count. Where the rogue corporation fails, Sully takes over. Cameron justifies the colonial enterprise by showing the natives living in a condition that makes Sully's intervention necessary. What plays out with this savior is the traditional logic of colonialism, which involves granting the high moral ground to Europe: Europe is selflessly invested in aiding and ameliorating the wretchedness of the Third World native. Sully's actions follow this model. For instance, in the scenes immediately following the attack on the Willow Glade, Sully cautions the Omaticaya about the dangers of resisting the forces of Quaritch without proper preparation. Here, he assumes the position of the colonial savior of the native masses. By warning an aggrieved Tsu'tey (Laz Alonso) against direct warfare, Sully saves the natives from an impetuous decision that could have led to their complete annihilation.

Sully's association with the Na'vi and his becoming a part of the tribe is achieved through violent representations of the

Na'vi as inferior. They are impulsive and childlike, but they can be also taught to be reasonable. The Na'vi share with children a lateral understanding of the connection between signifiers and signifieds. A man's intention can be tasted in his blood and a successful bonding with a Banshee opens membership to the clan. It is not surprising, therefore, that Sully's emergence as the leader of the Na'vi is founded on an act of wielding the Master Signifier, that is, of conjoining his body to the Na'vi myth of the Toruk Maktu. This act, as I discuss later, is a violent act of intrusion into and usurpation of Na'vi mythology. And what is the purpose of this act? It allows Sully to regain a toehold in the clan and emerge as their undisputed leader. The film provides a substitution of violent entrepreneurial intervention (RDA) with violent entrepreneurial intervention with a human face (Sully). The question to be asked is not which intervention is good, rather what gives either the RDA or Sully the liberty to represent the Na'vi, the indigene?

Can the Na'vi speak?

Accepting the award for "best director" at the 2010 Golden Globe Awards ceremony, Cameron thanked his actors and crew in the nonexistent Na'vi language and then translated what he said in English for the larger audience. In so doing he inadvertently exposed the truth about indigenous speech act. Cameron revealed the Na'vi cannot speak. At the heart of Cameron's performative speech are two gestures. First, when he speaks in the nonexistent Na'vi language to his actors, this suggests that all those who worked on the film know the language. Their presence guarantees their access to knowledge and renders the Na'vi present. Second, in translating the Na'vi words in English for the larger audience, Cameron appears to bridge a linguistic gap existing between the Na'vi and the West. Cameron interprets the Na'vi for the West. Cameron's speech renders the existence of the Na'vi and Na'vi language contingent upon the subject of the West. Therefore, Western subjective acts of translation constitute the Na'vi into being. That is to say, neither the Na'vi nor Na'vi speech can exist without, or outside of, the West. Embedded in the West's speech acts, the Na'vi is nonexistent. The primary function of Cameron's speech is to constitute the subjectivity of the West. The framing of the Na'vi in the speech (and the film) is a purely formal gesture. In the case of Cameron, the Na'vi establish his credentials as more than just a commercial moviemaker—as a blockbuster auteur who makes films on socially relevant issues.

Of course, Cameron's extra-diegetic performance does not necessarily indict the film itself, but what stands out is the extent to which it parallels the film. The Na'vi do not speak in the filmic universe either. This inability to speak does not mean the Na'vi cannot talk. It means Na'vi speech is either mediated by Sully, a subject of the West, or their speech makes possible, as background and through translation, the subjectivization of Sully as a Western subject. In "Can the Subaltern Speak?," Spivak gives the example of a young Bengali girl, Bhubaneswari, to explain the subaltern's inability to make their speech effectual. Bhubaneswari, Spivak tells us, commits suicide after failing to carry out the assassination of a British colonial officer. Even though Bhubaneswari decides to kill herself out of shame for failing the mission, she waits for her menstrual cycle to start so that her death is not assigned any other reason by society (unwanted pregnancy). In other words, she inscribes her message *in extremis* . . . in death and through her body. But as Spivak recounts, people (including those in her family) still fail to hear her speech, believing instead that she committed suicide to escape the shame of unwanted pregnancy. Spivak's point is simple: it is not that the subaltern does not speak, just that their speech remains incomplete, since the structures of hegemony cannot comprehend it.

The Na'vi remain virtual entities in the film. Depictions of indigenous suffering in the film are geared to draw our empathy leading to more calls for charity—the feel-good mantras of a multicultural West caught in an unending war of its own choosing. Unlike what pundits claim, by watching Cameron's film audiences learn nothing about the conditions of the indigene or about indigenous resistance against corporate exploitation. The film carefully excises indigenous voices alongside all possible references to ongoing self-contained indigenous armed struggles against all forms of capitalist operations. Subjects of Europe must always helm indigenous struggles, if they are to be effective, in Cameron's universe. As long as the condition of the indigene remains framed by a Western form of knowledge, that is as long as the indigene submissively folds into Western representations of agreeable Others, the West tolerates the indigene. However, when the indigene forcefully enact subjective acts of representation on its own, without Europe's political and moral mediations, as in the case of the Maoist movement in India, such acts are promptly categorized as terrorism, the indigene receives the label of "terrorist" and the Third World intellectual speaking about these movements appears unpatriotic.

Cameron's film scripts a manifest critique of colonialism while discursively incorporating into the scriptural space of the film the discourse of reformed enterprise. The new discourse does criticize the West's cultural or military interference in the non-West, but it does not dismantle the category of the West. The fantasy of the new subject emerges through enterprise of moral and physical labor to recuperate the image of the West without discarding the category of the West. In this new arrangement of capitalist realism, global capital reaches into the darkest recesses of the globe to touch the aggrieved subaltern and inscribe them in destinies written out from the vantage point of the West. But it is difficult to see how this ideological agenda unfolds in the recesses of Cameron's film.

"Father, don't you see I am burning?!" . . . "I See You."

Freud discusses the "Dream of the Burning Child" in *The Interpretation of Dreams*.[12] The dream tells of a father who has been caring for his ailing son but who falls asleep from exhaustion after the child's death. In the dream, the father sees the (dead) child appear next to his bed, alive, and whispering: "Father, don't you see I'm burning?" Awakened by the child's return and words of reproach, the father discovers that indeed his son is on fire: a candle had accidently fallen on the shroud of the dead child while he was asleep. Freud cites this dream to elaborate his theory that all dreams, including traumatic ones, has the purpose of prolonging sleep. He argues that the father smelled smoke in sleep, but instead of waking up in response to this external stimulus, he continued to sleep. And in this sleep he dreamt the image of the son's burning. Yet the father did eventually wake up. Jacques Lacan interprets this awakening as the father's attempt to avoid the trauma of encountering his dead child's complaints. The father wakes up in response to the child's insinuation that the Father is blind. Waking up is thus a disavowal of this trauma and the charge implied in the child's reproach, namely that the father had been uncaring of his child in life and contributed to his death.

When we read this dream alongside the story of Iphrat Koshen and his wife Mariam, characters in Palestinian writer Ghassan Kanafani's novella "Returning to Haifa" (1969), an interesting point regarding the imagining of the other's land as empty presents itself. In the novella, Iphrat and his wife are Polish Jews, survivors of the Nazi regime, who in the aftermath of the war have been temporarily relocated to Haifa where they wait for resettlement. At an important moment in the novella, the omniscient narrator lets us hear the inner voice of Iphrat. Looking out at the city from his balcony, Iphrat thinks to himself how he came to this new land:

> [He] couldn't even guess that he would come to live there. In truth, he believed that when things calmed down he'd go to live in a quiet house in the country at the foot of some hill in Galilee. He'd read *Thieves in the Night* by Arthur Koestler while in Milan; a man who came from England to oversee the emigration operation had lent it to him. This man had

> lived for a while on the very hill in Galilee that Koestler used as the background for his novel. Actually, not much was known about Palestine at that time. For Iphrat, Palestine was nothing more than a stage set adapted from an old legend and still decorated in the manner of the colorful scenes pictured in Christian religious books designed to be used by children in Europe. Of course, he didn't fully believe that the land was only a desert rediscovered by the Jewish Agency after thousand years, but that wasn't what mattered most to him then.[13]

Iphrat could well have read Homer or Darwin instead of Koestler. Even then he would have been conditioned to view and taught to desire the other land the same way. That is the function of ideology—to rearrange our desires.

But Iphrat is neither Odysseus nor Charles Darwin. He has been at the receiving end of a similar fantasy himself, a fantasy that not only deracinated the Jews but also expunged their right to land and nation. Thus victimized, he merely chooses to believe this promised land to be empty. It was what mattered most to him then. But the sight of a dead Arab child shatters his belief. During the tumultuous days of the *al-Naqba*, Iphrat and Mariam see Israeli soldiers unceremoniously throw the limp body of a dead Arab child into the back of a push cart to be disposed of somewhere later. This sight of the dead child haunts them: it makes Mariam want to leave Israel and return to Europe. It opens the couple to the scrutiny of the gaze of an unknown dead child and leads them to question the real stakes in imagining other worlds.

Iphrat and Mariam experience a similar trauma on seeing the dead body of the Arab child, as does the father in the "Dream of the Burning Child." Though the dead Arab child did not speak verbally, his lifeless body conveys a similar message to the elderly childless Jewish couple. In fact, the message conveyed by the dead children is one and the same: wake up because you can no longer sleep ignorant of our conditions; we are at your mercy. Both the children speak from the beyond, in death, capturing the addressees in their unerring gaze.

Not unlike the haunting messages writ large in the gaze of these dead children, the phrase "I see you" loops through *Avatar*. To see and to be able to see is an important motif in the film. While much has been written about what this means in a Western philosophical context—a critique of "phallocentric, dominant gaze" and privileging of Heideggerian *Umsicht* (or circumspect seeing) and highlighting of care for the (Levinisian) Other—one question has not been asked.[14] What if we imagine the phrase as one addressed to the viewers? What if it is a question from the indigenous Other to the audience asking if the latter can really see what's happening in the film? This is the unthought or unconscious of the film that exposes what Cameron means to hide: the Other sees the spectator, and yet the manifest content of the film does not permit the spectator to see this seeing.

The magnificent surface narrative about underdogs triumphing clouds spectators' judgment, making them lose sight of the text of subject-production in the film. The imaginary, feel-good reality of Cameron's film forecloses the real reality of global politics in the geopolitical present. Such foreclosures are deeply symptomatic of the (re)emergence of Eurocentrism in contemporary Western discourses. In Cameron's film and critical writings about the film, Eurocentrism develops in form of a repudiation of the otherness of the other. As Slavoj Žižek explains in his analysis of *Avatar*, "the film enables us to practise a typical ideological division: sympathising with the idealised aborigines while rejecting their actual struggle. The same people who enjoy the film and admire its aboriginal rebels would in all probability turn away in horror from the Naxalites [in India], dismissing them as murderous terrorists. The true avatar is thus *Avatar* itself – the film substituting for reality."[15] The film forecloses the real condition of subaltern suffering and indigenous dissent offering in its place a fiction of subaltern struggle beautifully packaged through CGI and 3D. The aesthetic marvel of the film is central to its colonial complicity: it enables spectators to admire what the colonized look like without seeing the possibility of their look (or the possibility of listening to their subaltern speech).

By allowing the film to mediate our understanding of the real conditions afflicting the indigene worldwide, we become ourselves complicit with the processes responsible for the suffering of the latter. The popularity of the film suggests that we find it comfortable to peer at real situations indirectly, through fantasy-scenarios, where violence of the oppressed is only acceptable under the guidance of a rational subject of the West. In light of this situation, we must tweak Žižek's contention that the film is the true avatar and say instead that the audiences of the film are the real avatars. For we participate in the film's virtual representations without wanting to engage directly with other peoples and their violent causes. The film sells the possibility of this virtual participation: audiences can root for the death of the US marines, enjoy the communion (and even sex) between species, champion the violent indigenous insurrection against capitalism, but then return to an everyday life supported by precisely the same kind of imperial exploitation that they enjoyed seeing destroyed. Like Las Vegas, which invites us to visit with the promise of secrecy, and video games where our avatars can engage in anti-social acts without us earning any disrepute, Cameron's film is another consumer product that facilitates our indulgence in anti-capitalist thoughts without having any repercussions for us in actual society. When it comes to confronting real issues besetting our social and political globalized realities we morph into virtual entities: we become humans bereft of will, capacity, and political consciousness. In fact, in today's global reality (which Mark Fischer terms "capitalist realism"), we transform into virtual avatars instead of joining strikes, protests, and agitations against the injustices of globalization. *Avatar* is complicit in the production of this "pervasive *atmosphere*, conditioning not only the production of culture but also the regulation of work and education, and acting as a kind of invisible barrier constraining thought and action."[16] Simply put, *Avatar* wants its audiences to consume and not question. It builds on the prevailing condition of gullibility and undecidiability of the West to conveniently pass a conservative, Eurocentric film as a film critical of Western materialism, expansionism, and corporate-militarism.

Scene II: the cultural production of messianic fantasy (re-presentation)

Avatar's narrative is punctuated by two blackout shots. One comes at the very beginning and the other at the very end of the film. The first blackout occurs when the film opens with a black screen, as sounds of drums come from a distance, growing louder as the shot fades in to show audiences a tropical forest canopy. The camera glides over the treetops shrouded in mist accompanied by a voiceover, that we later recognize to be Sully's. The voiceover says: "When I was lying there in the VA hospital, with a big hole blown through the middle of my life, I started having these dreams of flying. I was free." As the drums peak, the camera dips closer to the forest and the shot fades into a blackout with the voiceover saying, "sooner or later though, you always have to wake up." This is the first blackout. It dissolves quickly to show Sully inside a cryopod, shrouded in a metallic blue light, with his eyes shut. As the shot holds its extreme close-up on Sully's eyes, they suddenly open to stare back at the viewers.

The second blackout comes at the end of the film. As we wait anxiously for the migration of Sully's consciousness from his paraplegic human body to his avatar, the camera zooms to an extreme close-up shot of Sully's Na'vi face. The shot focuses on his closed eyes as it did in the beginning of the film, and, similar to the beginning shot, here too Sully suddenly opens his eyes to stare back at the audience. Immediately after he opens his eyes, the shot cuts to black.

Dana Fore has argued that everything that unfolds after the initial voiceover telling us about Sully's waking up in a VA hospital with a hole blown through his life and his recurrent dreams of flying and being free is a dream. The first blackout marks the beginning of "a dream of heroic struggle and ultimate redemption, where a monolithic war machine is destroyed by a handful of rebels in a hallucinogenic world where magic heals all wounds and disabled bodies disappear painlessly and permanently."[17] The second blackout ends this dream.

There is a certain logic to this reading. One can see how the film might be read as the dream of a disabled veteran who feels discarded by his own government and who wishes to avenge the wrongs suffered by him. But Sully's desire for revenge is spatially and contextually displaced. Dream or no dream, the displacement of action on a moon orbiting a planet roughly 4.4 light-years from Earth serves a definite ideological function. It tells the audience that no similar action is possible on planet Earth. Even if social conditions on real Earth mirror those of fictional Earth in the film, the ideological message is "don't try this at home; don't engage in militant dissent; don't organize the masses etc." In this sense, the fact that Sully's experience might be a dream does not mitigate the quietism of Cameron's film but actually augments the problem.

In any case, scenes edited from the theatrical release but available in the Director's Cut very clearly support Fore's hypothesis. In the Director's Cut, the initial blackout does not dissolve into the shot of Sully inside a cryopod. Instead, it opens with an extreme close-up of Sully's eyes but then backtracks to show him on a wheelchair waiting at a busy city crosswalk for the lights to change. In this shot, Sully is still on Earth, and events that follow depict his growing frustration with a society where the strong prey on the weak. Cameron poignantly establishes Sully's social isolation in this scene through the use of the close-up. Sitting in a wheelchair, he is dwarfed by the able bodied humans waiting alongside. The scenes following also show Sully's paraplegic body in clear juxtaposition with the bodies around him and on giant television screens. All throughout these scenes, we hear his voiceover complaining about returning veterans not getting medical aid pointing further to the isolation of people like him in a society run by rich corporations. In another shot of the inside of Sully's tiny apartment, we see the marine dwarfed by a huge television screen with a program running on it about scientists bringing the extinct Bengal tiger back to life. The voiceover in this shot passes from Sully to a television commentator whose documentary-style narration of the Bengal tiger news indirectly sends the message to the spectator about the validity of Sully's complaints. This society is technologically advanced to bring the extinct Bengal tiger back to life after a century, but it is indifferent about the social welfare of the masses, including its veterans. Sully's frustration in these edited scenes is palpable, and so is his desire to fight back—"All I ever wanted in my sorry-ass life was a single thing worth fighting for." Fore's thesis starts gaining critical relevance once we think of the film in terms of these deleted scenes. What follows between the two blackouts can be Sully's dream in which he travels to a far-off land, participates in a science mission that helps him regain his legs, and, finally, redeems himself against a

FIGURE 2 *Edited scenes showing Sully on Earth* (Avatar, *2009)*

system responsible for his real paraplegic condition and all-round injustices against people too weak to fight back.

Even though the blackouts function as non-diegetic filmic events, Fore interprets these as physical blackouts suffered by Sully within the filmic diegesis. She argues that the blackouts represent Sully's struggle to regain consciousness. Unlike Dorothy (Judy Garland) from Cameron's favorite film the *Wizard of Oz* (1939), Sully cannot find his way out of the dream world and continues to fall deeper into his fantasy losing all prospect of returning to reality. He fails to wake up. In Fore's opinion, this condition of inescapability makes *Avatar* a parody of inspirational films about war veterans, as it reminds audiences about the real suffering of US veterans in today's economic climate. The absence of a final image of Sully as a Na'vi furthers this effect. If audiences found it difficult to identify with a paraplegic hero at the start of the film, they are no better at the end when the film ends abruptly without showing Sully's physical wholeness. This interference with consumer satisfaction can be credited to the director. The film is a critique of our contemporary fascination with (maternal) wholeness, toned physique, and able bodies.

As such, the film gives its audiences the radical truth contained in the Greek myth of Pandora. That is, as Fore puts it, "hope is an unexpected kind of evil, one giving us faith in utopian promises and technological miracles while leading us further down paths of suffering from which there are no apparent escapes."[18] Fore's contention is that Cameron is a very different director than other Hollywood filmmakers. He is extremely sensitive about disability as a form of otherness and his scrupulous critique of the West's ableist, martial culture in *Avatar* attests to this thoughtfulness. It appears that Fore believes that even though most of Hollywood is ideologically aligned with global capitalism, there are still a few sensible voices in the industry courageous enough to criticize the West's unequal political policies and who seek to reform public opinion about cultural stereotypes instead of perpetuating these.

Unfortunately, Fore is deceived by the film's narrative and visual representations. While making a critical intervention in the reading of *Avatar*, her essay fails to recognize the ideology of subject-production that lurks behind the film's sensitive critique of ableist discourses. The focus of her entire essay correspondingly is on the production of truth and identity on the side of the West. The unconscious drama that Jake undergoes, even in her sympathetic reading, is a Western drama in which the colony acts as nothing more than a backdrop for the exploration of the Western unconscious. If the primary narrative of the film is just Jake's dream, this does not magically transform the function of the filmic fantasy but rather exacerbates the problem.

What Fore does not notice is that the Na'vi remain silent throughout. The silenced Na'vi function as the backdrop for the dialectical linking made in her essay between waking and sleeping and between knowing and not knowing. Fore contends that "waking up to see reality" and "failing to wake up to see the reality" exist as central tropes in the film. And these tropes constitute Sully's dream as well as his subjective condition in relation to his dream. This privileging of singular, epiphanic moments of ideological (or spiritual or sexual) awakening is used in the film to recuperate subjectivity at the expense of the Na'vi. Fore's reading of Sully's character in terms of the conscious and the unconscious overlooks the role these epistemic categories play in the narrative of subject-production, which is the fundamental preoccupation of the film.

Sully's character follows a traditional development arc, one that resonates with the discovery of a new true subjectivity that provides renewal. In this traditional arc, a seemingly contingent moment brings to light one's former ignorance and allows the subject of knowledge to constitute itself in the place of the unknowing. This changes one's subjectivity and engagement with the world. In the film, Sully's shifting of allegiance from his own people to the Na'vi is shown to correspond with a similar move from not knowing to knowing.

On the one hand, Sully grows aware of the real intentions of the corporation, and his first-hand experience with the bellicose, impetuous side of RDA during the Willow Glade destruction event convinces him to change sides. On the other hand, his growing disenchantment with RDA's policies is complemented by his growing knowledge (or, growing consciousness) about the Na'vi and their ways of life. Thus, as he gains more insight about life on Pandora by spending time with the Na'vi, he also moves from being unaware of the RDA's indiscriminate brutalities against the indigene to knowing and despising the RDA for its highhanded imperialist actions. The transformation in Sully's character pivots on experiences of contingent moments and conscious actions taken in response to these moments. Sully's transformation is the point of *Avatar*, and everything else in the film serves to inform this transformation. Cameron focuses on Sully and the change he undergoes through the aid of the non-Western Other in order to avoid allowing the otherness of this non-Western Other to speak. In the following sections, I explore two such critical instances—the Willow Glade destruction and the taming of the giant Toruk. Both are pivotal moments that the film employs to constitute Sully's subjectivity.

The Willow Glade incident

The Willow Glade incident stands at the middle point of the film narrative. It involves the RDA's razing of the Tree of Voices—a sacred site of ancestral communication to the Na'vi—and Sully's first physical act of resistance against the company. What comes after is the story of the RDA's assault on the Na'vi Hometree, Sully's defection, Na'vi resistance and victory over the human invaders. But what comes immediately before the incident is equally important. The Willow Glade incident follows the formation of Sully and Neytiri as a libidinal couple. In considering the Willow Glade incident, I will examine not just the incident of razing and Sully's

FIGURE 3 *The Willow Glade Destruction* (Avatar, *2009)*

resistance but also what comes immediately before—the formation of the libidinal couple—and what comes after the actual occurrence of razing—the attack on Hometree leading to Sully's defection.

If the destruction of the Willow Glade is a moment of critical recognition and absolute reversal (and thus central to the transformation of Sully's subjectivity), we will have to allow for the possibility that Sully did not know previously about the corporation's true intentions. The razing bulldozers convinced him for the first time about the cruelty of the corporation, a conviction that leads to his eventual betrayal of his own "race." Or even if he knew about the corporation's intent, he nonetheless expected the company to be less brutal in its treatment of the indigene. But how could a veteran marine with combat experience in Venezuela, a "mean bush," not know what role he and the other hired guns were expected to play at this interstellar outpost? And once on Pandora, did he not see the mobilization and the military hyper-masculinity on display? How did he miss the arrows stuck on the tires of the armored vehicles rolling past him? Did those not intimate him about things to come?[19] Moreover, in the orientation speech to the new recruits,

Quaritch had laid out in clear language the terms of engagement on Pandora:

> You are not in Kansas anymore ... You are on Pandora, ladies and gentlemen. Respect that fact every second of every day. Out beyond that fence every living thing that crawls, flies or squats in the mud wants to kill you and eat your eyes for jujubees. We have an indigenous population of humanoids here called the Na'vi. They're fond of arrows dipped in a neurotoxin which can stop your heart in one minute. We operate – we live – at a constant threat condition yellow. As head of security, it's my job to keep you alive. I will not succeed ... not with all of you. If you wish to survive, you need a strong mental attitude, you need to follow procedure.

Sully it appears was not listening nor looking. He was not yet awake to the realities of his new life.

Two scenes underscore his naiveté. The first occurs when he enters the avatar body for the first time, and the second when he enters the jungles of Pandora with Grace and Norm for the first time. In both scenes, Sully behaves like a child. He is initially amazed with his new avatar body and then with the plant life in Pandora's jungle. If his behavior on entering the avatar body can be explained as natural—excitement on regaining his legs—his actions in the jungle merit no such vindication. Amazed and surprised at the surrounding life forms, he lets his guard down as he rushes from one plant to the next—tapping the touch-me-nots, marveling at their luminescence and enjoying seeing them recoil at the slightest touch. While the scene makes for excellent haptic cinema, one would not expect a veteran marine entering an alien, foreboding territory to behave in such a manner.

These representations of Sully's innocence and gullibility are in fact rhetorical arrangements aimed at making the eventual change of his character more forceful and convincing. Sully's transformation from not knowing to knowing—from blindness to insight—contributes essentially to the film's ideological reimagining of his subjectivity. And though Sully did not shift sides because of a "local tail," it is not insignificant that the moment of his subjective transformation vis-á-vis the destruction of the Willow Glade coincides closely with the emergence of Sully and Neytiri as a libidinal couple.

Sully and Neytiri's interspecies communion signals a change in the discourse of the film. Their lovemaking in the presence of the ancestral spirits connected to the Tree of Voices constitutes a turning point in the film's narrative and the discourse of subject-production. The libidinal coupling of Sully and Neytiri helps to constitute the impact of the Willow Glade incident. The RDA bulldozers—machines driven by soulless and faceless RDA mercenaries—tellingly barge in on the Willow Glade arcade and the happily sleeping, recently mated couple. This rude intrusion by the invaders awakens the couple and signifies the audacity with which the RDA occupies even the most private moments in the lives of the natives.

Critics of the film interpret the formation of the libidinal couple in vastly different ways. Some argue that the romantic couple symbolizes a defiance of the fundamental impossibility of sexual relationship, while others read their figuration as deliberately binding audience attention to the fate of the couple in the looming conflict. As audiences grow concerned over the future of this new couple they grow more careless about the issues of class antagonism and economic inequality that beset the Third World indigene. What such explanations fail to register, however, is that the constitution of the libidinal couple silences Neytiri. In the post-coitus narrative of the film, Neytiri's function is limited to protecting and legitimizing Sully.

The film depicts Neytiri and Na'vi women in general as lacking agency outside their roles as mothers and teachers. Elisa Narminio and Matthew Wilhelm Kapell rightly note that "Neytiri is deprived of agency simply by being deprived of her voice. She is rarely granted an articulate speech by Cameron – she moans, wails, grunts, growls, hisses, screams – thus losing her agency while simultaneously emphasizing the emotive aspects of the feminine."[20] Initially, however, Neytiri does seem more articulate and forceful. Her more stereotypical features appear to develop after Sully and she make love. In the scenes following, we see Neytiri fight against Tsu'tey as the latter draws his dagger to decapitate Sully's disconnected avatar body. But most crucially, in the scene where Sully descends amongst the Na'vi atop the Toruk, Neytiri is the first to approach him and say, "I see you." She follows up this legitimization of Sully as their unquestionable leader with the confession, "I was afraid Jake – for my people. I'm not anymore." Even though her dying father gave *her* the task of protecting the people, in this scene she demurely relegates that duty to Sully.

It is useful to turn here to Spivak's reading of Charlotte Bronte's heroine Jane Eyre. Spivak uses the phrase "soul making" to describe Jane's plan of accompanying St. John Rivers to do missionary work in India. Once in India, Jane hopes to transform the lives of the heathens by helping the natives escape their oppressive religious and social strictures. Though this plan does not mature in the novel, Spivak argues for situating it logically in relation to Jane's social ascension through marriage with Rochester. Bruce Robbins further explains the crux of Spivak's point when he notes that Jane's desire to immerse herself in service to the Indian poor serves to abstract Jane from any aspiration she may have had for social accession and heteronormative social relations. In context of the novel's happy ending, this legitimizes Jane's "upward mobility" through marriage "as something more . . . than mere self-interested social climbing."[21] Bronte's female protagonist justifies the purity of her subjectivity by othering and employing the native women as prop.

Jake and Neytiri's interspecies neural consummation similarly reduces Neytiri to the existence of a prop. Like the other Na'vi, she is another rhetorical device serving the text's ideological function of subject-production and narrative progression. The Willow Glade incident and the coupling of Sully and Neytiri rhetorically arrange the rise of Sully as a self-reflexive, sensitive, liberty-loving white hero at the expense of the indigenous Other. Though Quaritch alleges that Sully betrayed his own race because he found a "local tail," "soul making" is more than finding a local tail. It is first and foremost about constituting the subject of Europe as the sovereign speaking subject. When Sully explains to Neytiri on one occasion that he is not an agent of the company because he is in love with her, this expression of love is in fact an expression of the emergence of a new kind of subject.

The rise of the Toruk Maktu

The story of the European subject is always contingent upon the hero undertaking a quest of incredible magnitude and lethal consequences. Though the exact nature of the task differs from text to text, the subjectivity of the hero is contingent on his success in a quest that tests his moral and physical limits.[22] In *Jaws* (1975), Brody (Roy Scheider) is pitted against the shark, which he must kill to save the beach; in *Die Hard* (1988), John McClane (Bruce Willis) must endure a battle with deadly thieves to save the hostages held at the Nakatomi Plaza; and, in *The Ten Commandments* (1956), Moses (Charlton Heston) must tackle each hurdle thrown in his way by the Pharaoh (Yul Brynner) before he can lead his people out of Egypt and into the promised land. Similarly, in *Avatar* Sully must tame the "last shadow."

The taming of the Toruk is the most significant act that Sully performs on the way to reconstituting his subjectivity. It is this radical messianic act—Sully controlling the extreme otherness of the Other—which finally helps him earn the absolute faith of the Na'vi. This is why Cameron leaves the actual act of Sully taking control of the Toruk unseen within the film. He shows Sully decide to take on the dangerous beast and then cuts to him coming to the Na'vi riding on its back and in control of the uncontrollable otherness (which even the Na'vi themselves cannot domesticate). As Toruk Maktu, he becomes their naturally anointed and long prophesized leader.

As the rider of the Toruk, he regulates Na'vi mythology, reserves the power to speak on the behalf of the indigene, and lays claim to their history. In other words, this valiant act of heroic quest is yet another symbolic act of violence silencing the Na'vi.

The power enjoyed by Sully through the taming of the Toruk is palpably captured in the scene where he descends from the sky atop the beast and amid the Na'vi. True to its name, "the last shadow" (that is the last shadow anyone sees) scene shows an ominous shadow passing over the Na'vi gathered in prayer. As the startled Na'vi look up at the sky in fear, the camera captures a dark blot against the bright light of the star Alpha Centauri A. The blot approaches closer to show Sully astride the Toruk. The scene captures the arrival of the prophesized Toruk Maktu, sealing Sully's place in the tribe as one who would save them from the threat of the invaders.

Apart from this visual presentation of Sully atop the leonopteryx, the shot also plays with the politics of verticality as a referential axis to power. As Kristen Whissel puts it, "recent blockbusters deploy a broad range of digital special effects to create . . . breathtaking imaginary worlds defined by extreme heights and plunging depths whose stark verticality becomes the referential axis of many narrative conflicts."[23] Verticality in digital special effects becomes a way of displaying power, but, according to Whissel, it also displays highly polarized conflicts. Sully's taming of the leonopteryx and his ability to chart verticality riding it not only fulfills his dreams of flying, but it also grants him absolute symbolic power over the Na'vi and the visual and narrative domains of the film.

This appearance of Sully hijacks Na'vi myth and history. His is an act of self-justification through an insertion into and occupation of Na'vi mythology. He gains power in this case not by essentializing the Other as different from or inferior to the self but by identifying with and occupying a place in the Other's symbolic universe. Without his drastic and insane move of capturing the Toruk, however, Sully had no other option left to him. Both the Na'vi and the humans had exiled him. "Outcast," "betrayer," and "alien" is how he describes himself prior to deciding to capture the leonopteryx. Alone on an inhospitable terrain, Sully needed to do something dramatic to find a way back into the human or the Na'vi camp. Capturing the Toruk was necessary for capturing the Na'vi imagination. The Toruk Maktu existed as an impossible figure in Na'vi mythology, and Sully's only chance of regaining his foothold in the Omaticaya clan was to insert himself into this impossible sacred space of the mythical. Without appearing in a way that Na'vi prophecy foretold, he could never have enjoyed the complete submission of the Na'vi.

Sully's infiltration of the Na'vi mythical imaginary is an act of usurpation of Na'vi history. From the moment he arrives atop the Toruk, he enjoys absolute control of Na'vi history: it will be a history written out by him and with himself as the subject. Sully will carve out a historical destiny for the Na'vi by leading them to victory in battle against a superior force. Henceforth, stories of the sixth Toruk Maktu will be told in Na'vi oral literature, and his deeds remembered by the generations to come.

This capture of Na'vi mythical and historical imagination, however, has a cost. It reorganizes Na'vi society and rewrites Na'vi political culture. Immediately after becoming the leader

FIGURE 4 *The outcast (*Avatar, *2009)*

FIGURE 5 *The rise of Toruk Maktu* (Avatar, *2009)*

of the Omaticaya, Sully collectivizes the separate Na'vi tribes in order to present a united front against a common enemy but this act also inaugurates his sovereignty over the entire landmass stretching from the jungles to the plains to the seas. The unification of the Omaticaya with the other tribes under the leadership of the Toruk Maktu figures this newly minted collective as a nation. A new political formation that develops on Pandora after the European model.

The role that Sully plays in constituting a large-scale political order on Pandora suggests that the indigene is incapable of imagining national communities and constituting themselves into social collectives. Clearly, the indigene does not have to wait—and would not wait—for the arrival of the West to lead it toward conceptualizing a political formation. But not in Cameron's film. In the film, Sully builds a nation and pits defiant chauvinism against Western imperial aggression, thereby reorganizing a binary identity politics and enabling the West to single out an Other for itself. This also allows us to expect a future in which human ways of organizing life end up reorganizing the Na'vi way of life. Already in the film, we see the Na'vi wielding RDA weapons. For example, in the scene where the humans are seen leaving Pandora, we see the Na'vi with terran guns in their hands. This means the Na'vi are already technologizing their society after the terrans. There's no telling what impact such technological derivations will eventually end up having on the Na'vi society as a whole. With Sully's anointment as the new Toruk Maktu, the implication is that he would be the ruler over all the different tribes, uniting them into a nation, and thereby securing for them a European political destiny. Or perhaps the other tribes will resist Omaticaya hegemony, which might lead the Omaticaya led by Sully and armed with human weapons to embark on a brutal repression of this dissent. In this vision of *Avatar*, the liberated Na'vi have a glib historical and political destiny shaped and categorized by Sully, who sacrifices his paraplegic body but not his war-mongering, Western consciousness. The departure of RDA does not signify the retraction of the human (or Western) influence from over Pandora. Once touched by the Europe, the other can never remain unaffected.

The textured and hierarchical social-symbolic of the Na'vi, the existence of which is attested by their rituals and socio-libidinal arrangements—the practice of selecting a future leader and the tribe's shaman and marking them out as future husband and wife, for example—are barely explored in the film. The culture of the Na'vi and the politics of that culture become secondary to their serving the Toruk Maktu's political vision of emancipation. The indigene transforms from the particular to the universal only by appropriating the West's desire for a collective identity.

The move from the particular to the universal is integral to the imperial narrative strategy of *Avatar*. This move has a long tradition in Western literature, and in Tasso's humanist rereading of Aristotle's *Poetics*, the move from particular to the universal is regarded as constitutive of the epic.[24] Cameron himself rightly sees *Avatar* as an epic but it should not be considered an epic only for its narrative scope, characterization, magnitude, and spectacle.[25] It is the trajectory of the particular becoming universal that locates it in the form. And Sully's taming of the leonopteryx is the singularly critical component that makes the film an epic. This act catalyzes a series of events in sequence which, beginning with the unification of the Na'vi and ending in their victory over the humans, function to fold a particular act of self-interest (Sully's taming of the Toruk) into an epic discourse about the new messiah. Simply put, the particularity of Sully's act becomes part of a universal history of liberation and freedom from violent oppressive regimes. Through this act, the particular becomes instantly universalized.

The plot of *Avatar* also bespeaks the universality of Sully's trajectory through its very banality. Many critics mocked the film for the tired storyline that it employs and teased Cameron for plagiarizing the animated film *Pocahontas* (Mike Gabriel and Eric Goldberg, 1995) while writing *Avatar*. But one must ask what this repetition signifies. It is not enough to say *Avatar* rehearses a clichéd plot. It is more important from a postcolonial perspective to ask why it does so. The answer is apparently simple yet deceptively complex. This repetition paradoxically attests to the existence of an insoluble leftover of the other that remains after every new clichéd symbolization of the Other has been completed. This remainder enjoins future efforts toward re-integrating the other-not-quite-symbolized only to end again with a part of the other escaping symbolization.

Homi Bhabha identifies this process precisely when he says that colonial stereotypes vacillate between the fixed, known, and hermeneutically sealed Other and something of the other that always evades successfully signification. But Bhabha leaves unexplained what this something is and what its character might resemble. I prefer to think of this fugitive, spectral other as structurally akin to what Jacques Derrida describes as a ghost that constantly returns (a *revenant*) and, to an extent, related to Spivak's subaltern. Existing as an aporia in the hegemonic discourse that traps the Other in its texture, the absent otherness marks the limit of colonial epistemology, thereby instantiating repeated attempts at knowing and controlling through knowledge. The incomprehensible, furtive other does not belong "to knowledge [or] to that which one thinks one knows by the name of knowledge."[26] It is the unsymbolizable, ugly, and unreadable and unnamable traumatic otherness of the Other. It lingers on as an anamorphic blot in and as an absence at the margins of the West's discourses, resisting signification and rupturing positive identity. As an impediment to subject-production it is the object cause of anxiety and that which continually drives the West's desire to symbolize the Other.

Scene III: making art out of a footprint! (spectacular)

Writing about the tenuous relationship between (digital) cinema and reality, Lev Manovich offers a simple yet poetic definition of cinema as "an attempt to make art out of a footprint."[27] This definition positions cinema squarely in relation to the founding text of Europe's colonial mythography—Daniel Defoe's *Robinson Crusoe*, and, in particular, to Crusoe's discovery of footprints on the beach of his barren island. Cinema has a close kinship with imperialism. The birth of cinema—the first screenings by Lumière and Edison in the 1890s—coincides with deaths of sovereign non-European nations—the setting up of the Congo Free State as the personal property of the Belgian King Leopold II in 1885 and the massacre of the Sioux at Wounded Knee in 1890. A significant part of Euro-American cinema has remained invested since in remaking unfinished imperial realities. These range from directly dramatizing imperial adventures (*Zulu* [Cy Enfield, 1964]) to allegorical critiques of imperialism (*Apocalypse Now* [Francis Ford Coppola, 1979]) to capturing anxieties over the colonial past intruding into the globalized present (*Caché* [Michael Haneke, 2005]). In the three films mentioned above, central male protagonists are plunged into situations outside their control, and in all three films they struggle like Crusoe to eventually overcome their individual subjective destitutions.

Today's Crusoe, though, is unlike the original insofar as he is not an individualist struggling alone on an island cut off from mainland Europe. The twenty-first-century Crusoe is a neoliberal (Western) subject living in a globalized metropolis and connected to the world via social media and the local Whole Foods market. She is vocal in protest against growing incidents of social injustices against minority communities, anxious about the West's neocolonial activities, and, at times, like Georges Laurent (Daniel Auteuil) the protagonist of *Caché*, haunted by "white guilt."[28] The most illustrative example of the global Crusoe is Elizabeth Gilbert (Julia Roberts) from the Hollywood film *Eat, Pray, Love* (Ryan Murphy, 2010). Frustrated with her life in the West, Gilbert travels around the world in search of the true meaning of life, and in the Other's space, she discovers sensory delight (Italy), spiritual fulfillment (India), and love (Bali). Her visit to these three sites gives her opportunities to reinvent and remake herself besides saving natives from regressive social norms.

Avatar obeys this same pattern. It remakes Europe by reminding it about Eastern spirituality and mysticism. The implication in the film is clear: in its unfettered pursuit of material wealth, the West has lost sight of its connection with Nature as a spiritual force. In *Avatar*, Pandora is a spiritual site that redeems the sins of the West. Like the natives in *Eat, Pray, Love*, the natives of Pandora can teach the foreigners lessons in the art of living. Westerners can learn to live closer to the natural world and overcome the alienation produced by unfettered capitalist production and consumption.

While Gilbert in *Eat, Pray, Love* makes use of this opportunity to revitalize herself, most of the humans in Cameron's film fail to take advantage of the opportunity for self-recovery that Pandora offers. They are only interested in Pandora's mineral resource and thus lose all prospects of reestablishing contact with their inner selves. Kimberly Rosenfeld perceptively summarizes this as she notes,

> In *Avatar*, Cameron shows us an Eden-like world, untouched by destructive human qualities, almost a post-nuclear refuge for people but with one caveat. Humans must abandon their capitalist values and reinvent themselves to cohabitate respectfully and harmoniously with their environment and each other. It is not innocent that Cameron chose to call this world Pandora. It's a world representing richness and gifts in the form of precious minerals, which will unleash the worst in humans as they seek to mine its sacred site.[29]

As *Avatar* shows, the Other space can produce very different reactions in people. Some may become worse while some may find connection with their spiritual selves.

The respective arcs of Quaritch and Sully's subjective development in the film clearly mirror this structure. Quaritch's character spirals down into a pure manifestation of colonialist brutality in its raw form, while Sully, through his championing of the Na'vi cause, seems an ideal subject for the geopolitical present. But in fact the characters represent the two attitudes that the Western subject takes up toward the Other—exploitation and sympathy. As Slavoj Žižek rightly notes, "beneath this sympathy for the poor, there is another narrative, the profoundly reactionary myth, first fully deployed by Kipling's *Captains Courageous*, of a young rich person in crisis who gets his (or her) vitality restored by a brief intimate contact with the full-blooded life of the poor. What lurks behind the compassion for the poor is their vampiric exploitation."[30] This metaphor of feeding on the Other's labor defines capitalism and the material conditions of the colonial enterprise, and manifests itself in some of the quintessential characters of European fiction like Prospero and Robinson Crusoe. Characters who incarnate the colonialist project.

Even though *Avatar* asks us to align ourselves with Sully and demonize Quaritch, the inclusion of Quaritch is necessary for the politics of the film. Spectators must be able to disavow the brutal exploitation of the colonized rather than simply identifying directly with the colonized through the figure of Sully. Spectators hate Quaritch in order not to see their reliance on the economic and political work that his attitude toward the colonized accomplishes for them. Though Sully is the film's hero, Quaritch is the point at which *Avatar* tacitly admits its political project.

A digital dystopia

The colonialist bent of *Avatar* appears not just in the narrative structure of the film or in the Other that it constructs but also in its atypical form. *Avatar* is a technological marvel, and one cannot separate Cameron's technological accomplishments in the film from the film's content. Admirers of the film argue that its technical accomplishments far outweigh its clichéd story. The technological brilliance leads Ellen Grabiner, Donald E. Palumbo, and C. W. Sullivan to rule out altogether the possibility of not enjoying the film. They say, "the lack of originality and subtlety in the narrative is, in fact, beside the point. Despite critical pans, one would be hard pressed to find anyone who has seen Cameron's technological breakthrough in 3-D and who claims not to have enjoyed the sheer visual delight of the thing."[31] They claim that this inescapable enjoyment resides in the way that *Avatar* constricts the gap between the screen and the audience. But other critics remain less sanguine about the technological achievements. These critics believe that the dazzling cinematic visuals misdirect audience attention from the film's "unremarkable qualities": "*Avatar* upholds the traditional notions of political leadership belonging to [white] men while the world of the spirit is women's [or Other's] dominion."[32] Not unlike the arguments over the film's ideological message, this conflict of opinions about the film's technological achievement constitutes yet another layer in the problem of reading the film. And while it is also common to dismiss or praise the technology of the film in isolation from or in spite of the film's political message, we must question the function of CGI in producing the filmic reality of *Avatar*. To that end, we can turn to two essays that deal with the relationship between digital technology and politics in *Avatar*—Adam Davis's "Native Images: The Otherness and Affectivity of the Digital Body" and Todd McGowan's "Maternity Divided: *Avatar* and the Enjoyment of Nature." Though these essays have very different theoretical orientations, both offer excellent insights into the use of digital technology in relation to the ideological underpinnings of the film.

CGI and animation are traditionally viewed as ancillary to photography and the human world. As a result, in films that combine live-action and CGI elements, the imaging processes exist in tension with one another. The CGI world of dinosaurs in *Jurassic Park* (1993) and the toon world in *Who Framed Roger Rabbit* (1988), for instance, variously threaten the photographic or human world, and for that reason these not-human worlds are abused, punished, or destroyed, in the end to reassert the rule of the photographic. The CGI or animation exists as an Other to the photographic world. The cartoon body offers a good illustration of this point. As a "repository [of] otherness," the toon body is, according to Davis, "mashed, battered, and stretched to capacity" and made to perform "its otherness within familiar discourses of difference (as in minstrelsy, in which black people were made to look buffoonish and dim-witted)."[33] Davis clearly uses the language of postcolonial and race theory to make sense of the political role that digital technology plays in the cinema.

According to Davis, *Avatar* is an exception to the rule. It stands in contrast to the prevalent mode of representation—that is, siding with the photographic against the digital—by carefully reversing this hierarchy of images to show the digital as no less affective or vital compared to the photographic. In Cameron's film, the digital resists the power and hegemony of the photographic. Thus, in yet another reversal of sorts, Cameron's film shows the photographic (and humans) and not animated dinosaurs invading the digital (and alien) world of Pandora. In the final battle where the technologies and cultures converge, the digital emerges victorious and thereby restores the dignity of CGI. And in the ultimate assertion of the privilege of CGI, Sully discards his photographic human image in favor of his digital avatar.

Davis reads Sully's avatar as critically bridging the traditional chasm between the photographic or human (read European) and the digital or the Other (read native) worlds. Sully's journeys between the two bodies—and between the photographic and digital images of himself—establishes the digital as not ancillary to but the equal of the photographic. Moreover, Davis believes that in the film the digital moves from its secondary position to the forefront through Cameron's bold presentations of CGI characters as protagonists, as making love on screen, and as defeating photographic humans. The film's representation of CGI destabilizes audience understandings of and expectations from the digital.

Remarkably brilliant as it is, the essay raises a few questions. The stark binarism that Davis establishes between images (photographic versus digital) and the worlds (terran versus Na'vi) proves problematic in the context of the film's depiction of a balanced ecosystem and the Na'vi connection to it as the main point of difference between the humans and the Others. This analogy situates the Na'vi as noble savages in possession of beautiful souls. The binary between the Na'vi and the terrans is a binary pathologizing the latter as incestuously murderous: the earthlings are marked out as having killed their Mother Nature. But even if the Na'vi come out on the positive side of the binary, the way that the film romanticizes the Other by envisioning them as connected to Nature actually contributes to the marginalization of the Na'vi. The Other exists as fodder for European subjects in need of revitalization, and they achieve this revitalization by feeding on those integrally connected to an imagined wholeness.

What is more, the emergence of digital technology itself bears the marks of the Western imperial project. Digital technology, as Philip Rosen argues, conquers already existing genres and regimes of imagination.[34] Digital images subordinate existing, older images to the digital regime. They transform historical reality into a malleable whole digitally unconstrained by historicity. This argument resonates with Davis's description of photography's treatment of the animated, on the one hand, and the representational manipulation of the colonized's lived realities in imperial discourse, on the other. At a structural level, all three—photographic, digital, and imperial—manipulations of an other reality involve the erasure of the space and time of the other. If the digital dissolves the prefilmic reality, then colonial discourses seek the denigration of the other's cultural and ontological heterogeny in order to allow for the creation of an image of the Orient. These erasures of what Rosen calls "preexistent facticity" constitute an empty space within which the representational narrative of Western imagination unfolds. This emptying out of history for the creation of a site open to reinscription is the fundamental condition required for all fantastic and radical imaginations of the self vis-à-vis the Other. It would not be wrong to claim that the digital and the imperial are equally wedded to utopian visions of a perfect world, and both require acts of physical or epistemic violence in order to realize these visions.

Photography and digital production have parallel relationships to the Other. Photography was the technology of the late nineteenth and twentieth centuries that justified colonial discourse through its representation of the Other. CGI is the technology of the late twentieth and early twenty-first century. The digital image does not require a referent and re-presents reality rather than representing it. But this does not divorce digital cinema from the logic of photography or from the rhetorical structure of twenty-first-century Eurocentrism.

No symbolic system is innocent of violent acts of exclusion and inclusion. The rhetoric of imagining other worlds as pristine utopias, even if to criticize the West, is a lingering motif in discourses of the West. Utopias are never products of free decisions but rather the result of forced imaginations. The utopian imagination is always a way out of a symbolic deadlock, but utopian imaginations are also almost always responsible for the death and the dislocation of real people. The material destinations at the end of utopian imaginations are never barren, never empty, and never uninhabited. They are always at the cost of the Other.

The most significant problem with Davis's defense of *Avatar* and its use of technology is its repetition of European entitlement. If we follow his premise that Sully's avatar bridges the photographic/human/Western world with the digital/Na'vi/non-Western world, we have to recognize that Sully's agency provides the basis for this bridge. Even when Sully transforms at the end of the film, he remains a human agent who is not fully Na'vi. He is Na'vi in shape and color but human in taste, in opinion, in morality, and in intellect.

Avatar is a recreation of Thomas Babington Macaulay's vision of ruling India with the aid of a class of Indians who would look like Indians but think and act like the English. Macaulay's argument pivots on the rhetoric of emancipating the natives from the shackles of an oppressive vernacular knowledge system by giving them free education in the English language about the Western sciences. But the underlying precept is a chilling logic for cultural genocide: to systemically eradicate vernacular culture and literature in order to recompose native symbolic reality after the model of the West. In a sense, Macaulay's was the first historical and material exercise in employing avatars to rule the empire.[35] Cameron follows with a minor revision: the colonizer goes native to repurpose his life as well as that of the indigenes.

Davis overlooks the film's situation in the imperial tradition of remaking the native through epistemically rearranging the native's socio-symbolic. He also fails to see the problematic role that Sully plays as the messiah in the film. The Na'vi, he writes, "don't need human intervention, but they do need Jake – his military skills, his rationalism and empiricism – to save them from human invasion and fill the hole in their own society that makes them vulnerable."[36] Davis believes that the natives need help from a rational subject of the West, but then at the end of his essay he comes to the conclusion that the film represents a key victory for natives. The postcolonial theorist should remind Davis about José Dolores's reason for refusing freedom from William Walker in Gillo Pontecorvo's *Burn!*—"If a man gives you freedom, it is not freedom. Freedom is something you, you alone must take." In any event, the emancipation that the film depicts is unsustainable. Once the colonizers leave, it seems hard to imagine that they would not return with larger and better-equipped forces, thereby eliminating the freedom that Sully has authorized.

A natural curse

Lush representations of Pandora and descriptions of Na'vi life as profoundly connected to Nature create an image of plenitude. The natural image of maternal bliss, corroborated through the presence-in-absence of the all-pervading Mother Spirit Eywa, constitutes Pandora as balanced, harmonious, and plentiful in contrast to a dead Earth. The respective ecologies of these worlds connect to their respective inhabitants further grounding the binary between the terrans and the Na'vi as almost naturally ordained. Todd McGowan contests this conventional argument in his essay "Maternity Divided: *Avatar* and the Enjoyment of Nature." He argues that far from presenting Nature as harmonious, the film actually dismantles the image of maternal wholeness by showing nature as constitutively split because it takes a position in the political struggle against the colonists. When Eywa chooses a side in the struggle between the terrans and the Na'vi, nature becomes politicized, alienated, and incomplete. The politicization of nature undermines the ideology of completion.

This assertion complicates a reading of the film in terms of binaries—Earth/Pandora, self/other, good/evil, and nature/technology. McGowan does not simply replicate a common, if fallacious, postcolonial assumption that the Other is already a part of the self, and all that needs to be done to resolve self-Other conflicts is for the self to recognize the Other as its most inner-most otherness. Rather, McGowan's reading is much more radical in its identification of the current ideological use of the image of nature's wholeness for suturing anxieties in Western society that is wholly alienated from the natural world.[37] Still, his discussion of Cameron's ideology-critique does not address the Na'vi, even though the essay recognizes the centrality of (nature's) otherness in the film's narrative discourse. Like Fore and Davis, McGowan too forecloses the Other question.

This lack notwithstanding, "Maternity Divided" is extremely useful in formulating an important postcolonial question: What does the politicization of nature imply for the colonized, the indigene, the other? Clearly, the Na'vi had a different idea about nature, because Neytiri tells Sully that the "Great Mother does not take sides; she protects only the balance of life." But the fact is that we see Eywa choose a side, and she does so in response to Sully's appeal. Sully is the agent responsible for politicizing Pandoran nature. But we must consider what this implies for the Na'vi. That is the postcolonial question.

The politicization of nature parallels other processes of imperial rewritings of the colonial culture and society. And like any other rewriting of the colony, a rewriting of colonial nature as political can serve the imperial imaginary and work to legitimize the Empire. This becomes apparent if we look at another analogous act of politicization of the colonized's culture—the imperial rewriting of *sati* or the Hindu practice of widow self-immolation. In British discourse, the practice of *sati* became a cultural signifier for describing the barbaric and regressive Hindu. Yet as postcolonial scholars such as Spivak, Lata Mani, and Rajeswari Sunder Rajan have shown, *sati* was not a universal practice in India but a localized, class-specific practice. Performed primarily in the British state of Bengal and only by the Hindus of the highest caste, it was motivated not by culture or religion, though both were invoked to justify the act, but for purely economic reasons.[38] In Bengal, where women had property rights, the practice of *sati* aimed at denying a widowed wife her share of the husband's property. *Sati* was a criminal act—a law and order issue. Eventually banned by law in 1829, the politicization of the issue saw the

British administration engaged in reading and reinterpreting the scriptures and the upper-caste urban Hindu society debating the pros and cons of the ban on *sati*. This political drama enabled the administration to selectively translate and codify what it claimed to be the scriptural laws of the Hindu past. The law itself contributed to British discourses of the colony as a culturally regressive space, the Hindu as engaged in barbaric acts of cruelty against their own women, and the Empire as the savior of the helpless indigene women.

The colonizer politicized the *sati*, but this had the effect of enhancing colonial authority. This is essentially the case because more often than not imperial politicizations of colonized culture and imperial culturalization of colonial politics function to rearrange sovereignty in terms advantageous to the ruling elite. This does not mean we step back from politicizing nature or indigenous cultures but rather that we obstinately and continually question the production of truth through these conceptual, social, and institutional spaces. As a result, we cannot stop where McGowan's assessment of Cameron's ideology-critique ends. As postcolonial theorists, we need to go further and ask about the ideology informing Cameron's critique of ideology. And what is the connection between this invisible ideology and the supposed political critique of the film? The political critique in *Avatar* functions as a renewal of the Western subject. It has nothing to do with the otherness of the Other that it depicts: this Other is there to facilitate a new imagining of Western subject formation. In the end, however, this remaking of the Western self is dependent on the abuse and erasure of the non-Western Other.

Scene IV: the *mise-en-scène* of the missed scene (specular)

In Mohsin Hamid's 2007 novel *The Reluctant Fundamentalist*, there is an intriguing sex scene. It describes Erika, a white upper middle-class girl from New York City, engaging in sexual intercourse with Changez, a Pakistani national working as an analyst for an elite Wall Street consultancy firm. An interracial couple in NYC is a familiar scenario, except in the novel this relationship is complicated by Erika's dead boyfriend, Chris. Constantly haunted by memories of Chris, Erika fails to reach any sort of intimacy with Changez unless the latter acts out Erika's fantasy. Erika wants Changez to pretend to be her dead fiancé Chris. It is only after Changez pretends to be Chris that Erica is sexually aroused.

One way to read this scene is to think of it as a spectral *ménage à trois*: though dead, Chris's specter joins Erika and Changez in love-making. And without the participation of the dead, there is no possibility of sexual intercourse between the living couple.[39] The scene tells us that sexual intercourse between the couple is not possible without an element of fantasy. That is, without the absent presence of the third, an additional element, a memory of unpleasure mediating their experience of pleasure, the couple (especially Erika) cannot experience any kind of sexual rapport. It helps Erika to stay connected to her past and to her dissatisfaction while enjoying a sexual act in the present. It is not that she does not know that Changez is not Chris, but Erika needs to see something more in Changez in order to engage in a sexual act. Their relationship gains meaning only in the virtualized presence of the dead that acts as an authority guaranteeing the meaning of acts (sexual or otherwise) in the symbolic order.

It is also possible to read the scene metaphorically. The scene is a harsh reminder of racial politics in the so-called post-racial world. Even for a liberal subject like Erika, communication with the racial, ethnic, Muslim Other is possible only when the Other's otherness is mediated through her dead white boyfriend. Only when Changez embodies Chris can Erika engage in sex with a racial Other. Otherness incorporated (or Otherness Inc.) is the fundamental way contemporary society negotiates racial, sexual, ethnic difference. Otherness appears as already inside the self; it is the most innermost part of the self hence and thus not distant or different. Or it exists as a fantasized exotic Other—a poncho bought at the local fair trade shop or a curry tasted at an Indian restaurant.

A postcolonial reading of the scene ought to highlight the failure of cross-cultural relations described through Erika and Changez's perverse sexual relation. The novel seems to be suggesting that East–West exchanges are impossible outside fetishistic fantasies of the Other and without the mediation of the past. The past in the case of Hamid's novel is the past of Western imperialism and a lingering ethnocentrism that symbolically manifests itself through Erika's necrophilic attachment to her dead white boyfriend. This reduces Changez, the historically trapped Other in the twenty-first century, yet again to the status of an imaginary surface aiding the production of Erika as a subject. The past constitutes their relation to the lived reality of the present, just as imperial history, which left few nations on the planet unaffected, continues to arrange present dispensations of global politics. Changez, on the one hand, is alienated between the past and present, between himself and the imaginary self of Chris, and, on the other hand, has no present but only the past as his reduction to a prop for Erika's gratification establishes him as a negated Other.

The Reluctant Fundamentalist depicts an alternative to *Avatar*. In Hamid's novel, the violence of the Western subject's interest in the Other comes to the fore, whereas *Avatar* obscures this violence through Sully's compassion for the Na'vi. And yet, his attachment to them requires every bit as much of a fantasy as Erika's in *The Reluctant Fundamentalist*. The difference is that *Avatar* shares Sully's/Cameron's investment in the fantasy of the Na'vi, while Hamid's novel takes up some critical distance relative to Erika's fantasy.

Leila Aboulela, another contemporary diasporic postcolonial author, presents the impossibility of East–West communication in the twenty-first century in a more stark and provocative manner in her 2001 short-story "The Museum." In this story, a love affair between a Scottish boy and a Sudanese exchange student fails because of their shared history of colonialism. Shadia, the exchange student from Sudan, tells Bryan, a white co-student from the coastal Scottish town of Peterhead, that she does not possess the strength required to endure Bryan trying to change his perspective on Africa. This is another story about the failure of cross-cultural communication between individuals from former colonial and colonized nations. The burden of history lies heavily on both Shadia and Bryan as they construct their respective cultural individualities and seek to transcend existing boundaries. But the formation of the two as a libidinal couple suffers at the critical moment of their encounter with the colonial histories of their respective nations. The museum in the story arranges the site of this present day cultural encounter. Against the backdrop of exhibits showcasing historical encounters between Scottish colonialists and the African colonized, Shadia realizes the impossibility of her relationship with Bryan. The historical narrative ritualistically contained within the institutional auspices of the museum and underlined by an anthropological-aesthetic cataloguing system describes Africa as an eternal metonym for colonial culture. This symbolic hierarchy could never support a relation of equality between Shadia and Bryan, not even with the latter promising to become more enlightened.

The lessons in Hamid's novel and Aboulela's story are simple—the narrativized hierarchy of colonialism continues to mediate everyday relationships between the East and West in the twenty-first century. Colonialism is alive even after its death, as its sphere of influence extends from the speech of the formerly colonized to the most intimate moments of lovemaking. On the other side, Western representations of the Other continue to be refracted through European pasts as nineteenth-century imperialism haunts contemporary constitutions of Western subjectivity and shapes its representational politics.

There is a similar scene of haunting in *Avatar*. Following the bombing of the Hometree, Colonel Quaritch orders the fleet to return to base. Immediately following, audiences see Selfridge, Max Patel (Dileep Rao), and a few others still gathered around a screen watching the destruction of the Na'vi settlement. The fleet transmitted the live video of the attack in real time, and during that time, spectators see a glimpse of the people at the base watching the attack unfold on a screen in front of them. But this second scene comes after the departure of the fleet from the site of the devastation. It leaves unclear as to who exactly is responsible for sending the latest video feeds.

This split-second scene captures those at the base as well as the spectator in the gaze. Properly speaking, no one is transmitting the video feed at this point, but the shot returns a gaze onto those who have been keeping an eye on the events. This gaze emanates from the site of devastation, recomposing a spectral eye that does not lose sight of the unfolding death for even a minute. It keeps sending back haunting images of suffering, desolation, and abject destitution of those bombed out of their homeland by the freelancing agents of the empire. What is worse, it entraps subjects complicit in this act as mere objects in the scene. The gaze catches the perpetrators of the crime as they look at and contemplate their heinous actions. The spectators in turn are exposed to the pathetic situation of Selfridge and others' witnessing the aftermath of the attack.

The shot also shows to spectators images that are often glossed, censored, and excised from representations of the wars of our times. The military operation by RDA in effect does not remain clean anymore. The cries of the dead and the dying, the images of mangled indigenous bodies, and the ecological disaster, disrupt the mastery with which Selfridge and Quaritch planned the attack. Though the military withdrew calling the operation a success, this gaze, surfacing at the exact moment when the imperial eyes shift from the scene, captures the empire as an unwilling witness to the real aftermath of the military invasion. The gaze resists, distorts, and ruptures the technocratic military-industrial gaze by giving body to the devastation left in the wake of the military operation.[40]

It has been argued that Cameron's cinema seeks to recuperate buried voices of the Other by challenging singular perspectives.

FIGURE 6 *Surveillance and the Gaze (*Avatar*, 2009)*

Through scenes like the one showing the indescribable suffering of the Na'vi in the immediate aftermath of the attack on the Hometree, he constitutes what a critic terms the "rhetoric of the Real."[41] If this is true, Cameron's attempts to revise history from below (literally in the case of *Titanic*, where the ship is underwater, and symbolically in *Avatar*, where the Na'vi are called *the people*) bring his films closer to the postcolonial emphasis on retrieving subaltern histories from the domination of European history. Read thus it would indeed appear that Cameron's film acknowledges the radical alterity of the other as constitutive of the self. But does he? Does the scene I mention above truly highlight images that are habitually hidden in media coverage of and populist discourses about the West's neocolonial wars? Is this scene accordingly emphatic proof of the film's anti-war character and the director's anti-colonial sensibilities?

I believe otherwise. The problem with critical commentaries crediting Cameron's film for highlighting the cause of the Third World indigene is that these fail to account for the role that the images of destruction in the film play in Sully's subject formation. Cameron carefully manipulates the gaze in this scene. Yes, the shot shows the plight of the indigene as victims of corporate-militarism and neocolonial violence, but it says nothing new or nothing that we do not know already. The images of dying indigene do not open up a hidden reality shocking the audiences to an epiphanic realization of the contemporary reality of war. If anything the scene repeats what we already know or suspect to be true.

A group of artists recently attempted something similar in the Khyber Pakhtunkhwa province in the northwest of Pakistan.[42] On the rugged landscape of the region, which is also a site of frequent drone attacks, the artists installed a giant poster of a young girl's face looking upward at the sky. The artists worked under the belief that the sight of an innocent human child looking upward at the skies would help drone operators realize that their victims are not bug splats. The poster is an excellent attempt at harnessing the power of the gaze. Commonly regarded as bugs from the grainy videos of their bodies as seen through the eye of the drone, the poster of the girl with her big eyes turned up at the skies assaults the drone operators by looking back at them. The installation uses the girl's gaze to objectify the drone operators, thereby radically rupturing the latter's habituated "experience [and exercise] of imaginary mastery" over the scene by converting that experience to "a traumatic encounter with the Real."[43]

That is to say, the installation project attempts to make the virtual into real. Or what appear unreal—real humans as pixelated images resembling bugs—becomes an identifiable human face through this project. The human that the technocratic look of the military could not see becomes visible as a gaze that sees and disrupts the military's omnipotent look. The project, though, depends for its success on the conviction that US soldiers, on seeing a human face, would awaken from their brainwashed stupor. The girl's imploring eyes would revive the soldiers' conscience, and they would refuse to perform the commands of the military-industrial complex.

At one level, the entire rationale anticipating the success of this project is structured by the association of consciousness to knowledge and a corresponding identification of not knowing with the lack of information. According to this way of thinking, the rational human subject is one who is in possession of knowledge and the irrational human subject is one who lacks knowledge. Without an influx of knowledge, the irrational and unthinking subject cannot transcend her state of not knowing to become a fully rational subject. This division of the human subject in terms of the binary of knowing and rational versus not-knowing and irrational is a mode of thinking entrenched in Enlightenment humanism. Colonialism employed this same logic during colonialism to legitimize European occupation of less sentient natives. Moreover, the structure of this binary map of identity pivots on knowledge, and this knowledge is always European knowledge or the knowledge of the European.

The division of the human subject into those who know and those who are unknowing ignores what, following Freud's discovery of the unconscious, stands as "unacknowledged knowledge." Freud describes the unconscious as knowledge that does not know itself—that is, knowledge that we do not know we know. Colonialism is not the result of an absence of knowledge. Colonialists knew what they were doing, and similarly the production of the East as the Orient came about not because of any lack of knowledge about the non-West, but as a result of repressed, foreclosed, and disavowed knowledge about the Other. That such habits continue to underwrite contemporary interventions into and imaginations of the non-West is attested by essays like Fore's (which I discuss above) and the art installation in Pakistan.

Knowledge is not objective. The success of the installation project in Khyber Pakhtunkhwa is conditional on the knowledge of the command to not kill. The project thus reinscribes a traditional moral structure to restrain US soldiers from killing innocents. It hopes that by awakening their religious conscience the drone strikes would stop. In effect, the entire project ends up substituting one ideology for another. It doles out a moral and religious opiate to help withdraw from a technocratic military-capitalist fix. The Khyber Pakhtunkhwa art installation, like Cameron's film, is astounding in its conception and brilliant in its execution. However, it does not engage with the real reasons for the conflict.

US soldiers are not unaware of the lives lost in neocolonial wars, and the spectators who watch *Avatar* are not simply unknowing about imperial violence and suffering in the colony. Thus, exposing this suffering does not function as a panacea. It actually enables spectators to enjoy the suffering by pretending to identify themselves with the victims of the wars from which they are the direct beneficiaries.

The *mise-en-scène* of violated and wounded bodies of the subaltern make the attack on the Hometree real. But whom do these sights of death and dispossession really affect? If we consider the filmic diegesis, there are not many people other than Max Patel and the Scorpion pilot Trudy Chacón (Michele Rodriguez) who seem to be affected by the sights. Both defect as a result to Sully's side. It is important to keep in mind, however, that both Patel and Chacón were already marginalized figures in terms of race and gender. Trudy, a woman in a man's world, and Patel, a scientist of color within the closed white military-industrial complex are outsiders and outliers from the very beginning. It is hardly surprising that they both end up defying the military-corporation. Given their already marginalized positions in the RDA, if the attack on the Na'vi Hometree had not worked as a trigger, something else would surely have. To return to my question then: who does the scene really affect and to what purpose? If it is no one in the film, then that leaves the audiences watching the film.

Ideologically speaking, the scene functions to shift audience sympathy toward Jake Sully. It builds audience pathos to aid the subsequent emergence of Sully in the film script as the messiah of the oppressed. The presentation of Sully as the leader of the oppressed also functions to mitigate the uncanniness and trauma of this shot of devastation. The fantasy of Sully leading a subaltern insurrection against imperial aggression is the stuff of dreams: it articulates conditional hope for the wretched of the Earth. This hope lies only through submission to the white man's fantasy. The subaltern can choose between direct imperial violence and submission to the colonial messianic fantasy.

In the scenes that follow the massacre of the Na'vi during the RDA's attack on the Hometree, Sully is shown to single-handedly assume the responsibility for building the Na'vi's political consciousness. He organizes the various segregated tribes into one composite whole; thereby linking the remaining disjointed parts of the Pandoran biosphere into a cohesive sovereign sociopolitical organism. In a sense, the Na'vi were not truly in connection with their world till all the tribes united. It is only after Sully joins the separate Na'vi tribes under the hijacked signature of the Toruk Maktu that the Na'vi for the first time really connect to their world. Na'vi society becomes a true reflection of Pandoran nature fulfilling what is essentially an Enlightenment dream of founding the social state on natural law. Interpretations of the film emphasizing Pandora's ecological interconnectedness and biotic kinship between the Na'vi overlook how the potential of this interconnected biosphere had remained unrealized till the intervention of Sully.[44] Sully tames the Toruk, unites the tribes, and politicizes Eywa. While the maternal presence of Eywa allows for the existence of such a connection, it was Sully as a paternal figure who successfully executed the command that leads to the unification of the tribes and the first complete connection between all the entities on Pandora. Pandora was an empty land with extraordinary potential but none of that was successfully harnessed until the arrival of Sully. The tribes and the animals and Eywa connected integrally for the first time through the labor of Sully.

Images of the subaltern (or Na'vi) anguish in the film are just that—images. Empty and one-dimensional, these occasion the soul-making and subject-production of Sully. These images metaphorically reorient the white man's burden and reclaim the white man's actions as a sign of the West's continuing sovereignty. The West is to remain the historical agent driving the global future, just as the subalterns are to remain the tools, props, and backdrops for designing and anointing the West as the master of history. The subaltern forms the imaginary-symbolic axes indispensible for mediating the West's arrival on the global stage as a conscientious, self-reflexive subject, and for rekindling in the West a desire for its history-making revolutionary subjectivity. The West today must remake itself in its image to negotiate the clash of civilizations and usher in another end of history. What is required of it is yet one more effort—another act of repetition through another opportunity to revitalize itself by feeding off the Other.

The film should have ended with the shot of devastation—a shot that shows the indigene massacred by First World mercenary forces. This is the history of neocolonialism, just as much today as before. In October 1988, Frantz Fanon's daughter witnessed protestors, mostly Algerian youth, in the El Bair district of Algiers being shot down by the forces of the state. At that moment Josie Fanon could only remain a mute witness. Later, she tried recounting her horror to the Algerian novelist Assia Djebar, but all that Josie could exclaim over the phone to her friend was: "Oh, Frantz, the wretched of the Earth again."[45] In the global present, the predicament of the liberal-bourgeois and the proletariat is to remain mute witnesses. Hollywood eases this stifling condition by offering alternative avenues for sympathizing with and championing the causes of the wretched of the Earth without actively joining their ranks. *Avatar* leaves its spectators satisfied, feeling hopeful that we have noted the plight of the historically oppressed and that we have adequately criticized the West's responsibility in the matter. The real condition of the indigene remains either unregistered or, far worse, gets eventually folded into the axioms of Hollywood's endorsed forms of protests. This is ideology at work in its most pragmatic form.

Cameron's contract

In the preface to Lisa Fitzpatrick's *The Art of Avatar: James Cameron's Epic Adventure* (2009), Cameron says that the phrase "suspension of disbelief" best describes the relationship between a filmmaker and her audience. This unspoken contract supposedly suggests that audiences go to the cinema with the knowledge that what they watch is "nonsense" yet they are willing, Cameron claims, to "forget about that for a couple of hours" and "have some fun."[46]

This characterization of the audience–filmmaker relationship recalls the paradoxical logic of fetishism—"I know very well, but nevertheless." To describe this phenomenon, Freud explains that a fetishist knows very well that the object of his desire is not the original maternal body part or object signifying it, yet the fetishist still invests all his sexual energies in pursuit of and enjoying this object. He does this to evade encounter with castration or learning the truth of the mother's lack. Postcolonial theorists like Edward Said and Homi Bhabha show how a similar logic of fetishistic disavowal structures imperial representations of the native Other. In neocolonial self-righteous discourses, however, it is the opposite. Cameron can openly make an honest admission about the real purpose of his films by telling his audience that "I give you three hours of cinematic time to live out your fantasy, that is, in this time your dirtiest innermost wishes, including seeing marines killed in a Third World insurrection, can be unrestrained." The implication of the contract is clear. Once the three hours have passed and once the audiences have stepped out of the theater, they are not to indulge the dissenting Other. They are not to join striking workers demanding living wages nor are they to endorse the Maoists in India fighting for the rights of India's tribal populations. The destiny chalked out for the masses in the twenty-first century is to remain caught between universalism and globalization with no real vocation for the particular allowed. In the words of Jacques-Alain Miller, this is the United Symptom of the twenty-first century.

Gayatri Spivak captures the condition of the twenty-first-century liberal-bourgeois pithily when she says in an interview with Robert Young that neocolonialism encourages the idea of the revolutionary tourist. But one "can't just be the Savior of the world on your off days," she cringes.[47] Neocolonialism continues to promote cultural relativism—the recognition of cultural difference but an almost willing misrecognition of power relations in-between different cultures—to subsume all subjects, with or without their knowing, into being complicit with the processes of class apartheid. The twenty-first-century metropolitan subject or the global Crusoe is conscious about the systemic corporate violence against the global indigene. We see this subject in various protest marches, and, if unable to march, then passionately voicing their concern on social media. Yet, at the same time, this subject is unwilling to admit that capitalist exploitations of the indigene cannot be countered without armed resistance. The exploited indigenes are allowed non-violent modes of protests but not violent insurrections against transnational corporate conglomerations and their comprador national institutions. The emancipatory anti-capitalist politics of the metropolitan bourgeois subject encounters a limit at this radical edge of contemporary indigene politics. Cameron's film is the perfect panacea for these people. To them, the fantasy of natives with bows and arrows resisting technologically advanced military forces with the help of primordial nature spirits and a renegade white man appear more probable than an actual armed resistance on the part of the indigene. Little do they want to understand that the liberation sought by the indigene cannot be achieved without a violent rewriting of the reality established by capitalist hegemony, years of colonial structural oppression, and morbid values of bourgeois morality. Indigene acts of resistance are not only directed at an immediate identifiable enemy but also at a semiotic system responsible for material and epistemic oppression of the indigene. Cameron's film not only allows audiences to sympathize with ideal indigenes while overlooking their real struggles, but it actively strives to teach audiences to decouple epistemic oppression from physical oppression by showing the RDA in the most caricaturist manner. Depictions of the soulless, absolute evil RDA agents, who like Quaritch can even withstand inhaling Pandora's poisonous air, carefully conceal Sully's epistemic acts of violence against the Na'vi. This separation of the physical acts of violence from the epistemic acts of violence allows the liberal-bourgeois to abstract themselves from the material forces of capitalism—the corporations, hired armies, corrupt politicians, and industrial lobbies. It enables the bourgeois in the global metropolis to continue feeling relevant by posting Facebook updates about Monsanto's terror or by debating the rights of terrorists. Yet what remains hidden from these virtual revolutionaries against global oppression is their complicity with global capitalism. Their noncommittal attitude is purposed into the workings of and solicited by an immensely fecund capitalist system.

Indigene revolutions (and all revolutions for that matter) almost always become violent, ugly, and traumatic because they replace the virtual with the body. Liberation is never a spontaneous act nor an act of self-discovery as Cameron's film attempts to promote. The indigenes in India who have taken up arms have done so only after their repeated attempts to seek social redress failed. Spivak reminds us that subalternity is a condition marked by two corresponding and concurrent aspects of hegemonic negation: first, the separation of the subaltern from structures of social redress, and, second, the delegitimization or constitutive alienation of the subaltern's struggle for social redress from all other forms of constitutional struggles. With access to the legal, the executive, and the judiciary barred by a government working to actively accommodate the demands of multinational corporations for land and cheap labor, the subaltern has no other option but to take up arms. A violent state and its hegemonic scaffolds cannot be countered simply with nonviolence.

The greatest adversary of the indigene are not the forces of the repressive state apparatus, but the sympathizers who advocate their cause on Facebook and donate to charities for quick resolution of their travails. The problem with these supporters is that they come with their humanist moral baggage.

Cameron's film offers a buffer against encountering the real conditions of indigenous liberation wars alongside satisfying the bourgeois need to empathize with the indigene Other. By rooting for the defeat of the marines at the hands of the indigene, audiences can, within the relatively safety of a dark theater, fulfill their moral obligation of protesting against US imperialism without having to assume the radical extent of rallying furiously against the corporate-state nexus or supporting the indigene engaged in armed revolution against multinational corporations. In celebrating *Avatar* we say "we didn't know about the condition of the indigene exploitation before, but the film has brought it to our attention," when what we mean is "we know very well what is happening throughout the globe, but we chose not to talk about it . . . because we do not want to get sucked into endorsing the armed indigene war." The least we can do today is to confront our own ideological perversions before hitting the streets for a protest march or pressing the "like" button on social media from the relative comfort of our homes to object against the oppression of the indigene in the global South.

Cameron's intent in making a film that mediates a safe ideological position for his audience is clear from his interviews.

Talking about his journey to the Amazon to raise public awareness about the adverse effects that the construction of the Belo Monte Dam on the Xingu river will have on the native tribes inhabiting the area, Cameron states that he does not advocate that his audiences leave the cities and go to live in jungles among the Kayapo (an indigenous Brazilian tribe). While he enters tribal villages anointed as their "new warrior," he cautions his audience that joining the tribes against the Brazilian government is not the solution. But then it is not for the Brazilian government that he speaks but for the Kayapo who "don't want us there." In addition, he claims, it is impossible to return to tribal life because we have lost our connection to "ancient knowledge." I am not sure what this "ancient knowledge" is or was, but I do recognize religious revivalism when I come across it. Cameron's notion of a golden past from which we have now fallen fits squarely in that domain. But then a Hollywood Marxist director of blockbuster science fiction films always carries a futurist card up his sleeve. In this case, he clarifies that all we need to do in the present is to transform ourselves "into something that's never existed on this planet," namely, "a kind of techno-indigenous people."[48] Cameron asks his audiences to remain attached to a technologized way of life while devoting some of their time to sympathize with the indigene in the global South. That is, he asks us to remain technologically committed to the indigene cause without committing our bodies to the struggle against capitalist exploitation of the indigene.

Cameron's ability to sound intellectually relevant and politically committed explains his appeal with the university educated left-of-center populations. Speaking to Marguerite Suozzi of Inter Press Service (IPS News Agency) on the sidelines of the screening of *Avatar* at the 9th session of the United Nations Permanent Forum on Indigenous Issues, he says:

> I think people have to distinguish between African American issues in this country where it's socioeconomic issues dealing with poverty and a voice in the political system, a place at

> the table . . . versus actual survival when bulldozers are knocking down your forest and you have a highly mechanized, industrialized force that's destroying your world. When all you've got to *fight back with is bows and arrows, there has to be intervention from the international community. . . . We have to help these people because you can't stop a bulldozer with bow and arrow.*[49]

Cameron here clearly states that *Avatar* is not a film about all and every community marginalized, harassed, and systematically exposed to neoliberal state violence. It is not about every minority group gaining political representation or identity rights, but it is about the survival of the poorest of the poor, the subaltern, the indigenous populations of the globe. He uncannily echoes Spivak's warning against applying the term "subaltern" indiscriminately to all and any marginalized groups. Yet what is conspicuously absent from Cameron's view as well as in the film is any engagement with elaborating the conditions responsible for silencing the subaltern-indigene. Instead, Cameron moves in the interview toward romanticizing

FIGURE 7 *Cameron plays the savior (special feature "A Message from Pandora," extended collectors' edition of* Avatar, *2010)*

the subaltern and its resistance against neocolonialism. Cameron's indigene is technologically stuck in the medieval age. They fight with bows and arrows against a highly mobile and technologically sophisticated adversary. Cameron, who is known to research his plots extensively, never for once refers to indigene fighters who resist the bulldozers of neocolonialism with automatic rifles and incendiary bombs. He chooses to conveniently omit these struggles for self-representation from his references to indigene resistance. Not unexpectedly Cameron wants his indigene to remain nonviolent. Though he craftily couches this demand in a rhetoric that appears to suggest that acts of violence might prove disadvantageous and fatal to the indigene, what he implies truly is that the indigene should not take up arms to counter state violence. He asks the indigene to seek redress at courts that constitute the very axiomatic structures of the governments that oppress them. In an interview with *Democracy Now!* Cameron says:

> There have been incidents in Peru just recently where . . . guns were used on protesting indigenous people, who fought back with bows and arrows, and death on both sides. . . . In order to forestall future violence and bloodshed . . . we have to be having this dialogue [facilitated by his film, of course] because these people [i.e., the indigenous] are informed enough . . . to know they . . . have a moral and ethical basis for their fight, but they also have a legal basis.[50]

Cameron's indigene must remain aggrieved but without the material means of protest until the First World rational subject appears in their midst to listen and guide them towards a resolution.

"Forestall" is a key word in Cameron's plea—and it underwrites the logic of *Avatar*. *Forestall* in Old English means "to stall" and "to buy up in order to profit." In Middle English *forstal* means "an act of way laying." The Oxford English Dictionary defines "forestall" as "an ambush," an "intercept." None of these etymological hints should be lost when considering how *Avatar* prohibits the subaltern from asserting its rightful anguish in a language that is both "heard" and "understood" by the state. Sully becomes the anointed leader by ambushing the Na'vi, first gaining entry into the tribe and the heart of Neytiri through deception, and, then, courageously and miraculously taming the leonopteryx. His eventual rise amongst the Na'vi represents the colonization of the Other by a subject who looks like the Na'vi but is European by consciousness. As Katherine Hayles sees it, the Western liberal subject possesses a body but is not represented as being a body. Erasure of physical embodiment is thus a feature common to the liberal humanist subject.[51] *Avatar* is a fantasy about ceasing to be white without losing white privilege.

Notes

1 These assessments are so commonplace that it would be impossible to review them all here. To cite just a few, see David Brooks, "The Messiah Complex," *New York Times* (January 8, 2010): http://www.nytimes.com/2010/01/08/opinion/08brooks.html; John Podhoretz, "Avatarocious," *The Weekly Standard* 15.15 (December 28, 2009): http://www.weeklystandard.com/Content/Public/Articles/000/000/017/350fozta.asp; Ezili Dantò, "The *Avatar* Movie from a Black Perspective," *Open Salon* (January 4, 2010): http://open.salon.com/blog/ezili_danto/2010/01/04/the_avatar_movie_from_a_black_perspective; Nagesh Rao, "Anti-imperialism in 3D," *Socialist Worker* (January 7, 2010): http://socialistworker.org/2010/01/07/anti-imperialism-in-3D; Carlos Quiroz, "*Avatar* is Real," *Green Left Weekly* (January 24, 2010): https://www.greenleft.org.au/node/43088. For a more scholarly critique of the film, see Dominic Allessio and Kristen Meredith, "Decolonising James Cameron's Pandora: Imperial History and Science Fiction," *Journal of Colonialism and Colonial History* 13.2 (2012): http://muse.jhu.edu/login?auth=0&type=summary&url=/journals/journal_of_colonialism_and_colonial_history/v013/13.2.alessio.html.

2 See Todd McGowan, "Maternity Divided: *Avatar* and the Enjoyment of Nature," *Jump Cut* 52 (summer, 2010):

http://www.ejumpcut.org/archive/jc52.2010/mcGowanAvatar/; Dana Fore, "The Tracks of Sully's Tears: Disability in James Cameron's *Avatar*," *Jump Cut* 53 (summer, 2011): http://www.ejumpcut.org/archive/jc53.2011/foreAvatar/; and, Adam Davis, "Native Images: The Otherness and Affectivity of the Digital Body," *Jump Cut* 55 (fall, 2013): http://ejumpcut.org/currentissue/DavisCGI/index.html.

3 Gayatri Chakravorty Spivak, "Can the Subaltern Speak?," in *Marxism and the Interpretation of Culture*, eds Cary Nelson and Lawrence Grossberg (Urbana: University of Illinois Press, 1988), 276.

4 Alexander Etkind, *Internal Colonization: Russia's Imperial Experience* (Hoboken: Wiley, 2013), 94.

5 For the use of the idea in Nazi doctrine and its links to the rhetoric of American wilderness and the Westward expansion of the US, see Roderick Nash, *Wilderness and the American Mind* (New Haven: Yale University Press, 1967); Annette Kolodny, *The Lay of the Land* (Chapel Hill: University of North Carolina, 1975); Robert L. Nelson, ed., *Germans, Poland, and Colonial Expansion to the East: 1850 Through the Present* (New York: Palgrave Macmillan, 2009); and, Carroll P. Kakel, III, *The American West and the Nazi East* (London: Palgrave, 2011).

6 Homer, *The Odyssey*, trans. Robert Fitzgerald (New York: Alfred Knopf, 1992), book IX, lines 110–121.

7 Charles Darwin, *The Descent of Man* (London: Penguin Books, 2004), 689.

8 For more basic information about the film, see Maria Wilhelm and Dirk Mathison, *James Cameron's Avatar: An Activist Survival Guide* (New York: Harper Collins, 2009).

9 I borrow the phrase "phonetic glue" from Mavis Himes. Following Jacques Lacan, Himes calls proper names the phonetic glue of identity. According to him, proper names attach a distinct historical/cultural/ political identity to individuals. See Mavis Himes, "The Weight of the Proper Name" (Book Review), American Psychoanalytic Association, Division 39 (Spring 2012): http://www.apadivisions.org/division-39/publications/reviews/the-proper-name.aspx. The importance of the proper name is also weaved into the very texture of Homer's book IX. At this point

in *The Odyssey*, when the Phoenician king Alkinoos asks Odysseus to reveal his identity, he says, "I am Laërtes's son, Odysseus." The name then plays a significant role in the story of Polyphemus. In order to facilitate his escape, Odysseus tells Polyphemus that his name is "Nobody," but when he finally escapes Polyphemus's lair he cannot resist calling back, "Kyklops if ever mortal man inquire / how you were put to shame and blinded, tell him / Odysseus, raider of cities, took your eye: Laertes' son, whose home's on Ithaka!" Homer, *The Odyssey*, book IX, lines 525–529.

10 Reena Dube, *Satyajit Ray's The Chess Players and Postcolonial Film Theory* (Basingstoke: Palgrave Macmillan, 2005), 11.

11 This is not the only reversal. Like Gillo Pontecorvo's *Battle of Algiers* (1966), Cameron's film inverts the imagery of encirclement. In addition, by positioning the humans as invaders from outer space, the usual narratives of alien invasion, such as *Independence Day* (Roland Emmerich, 1996) and *War of the Worlds* (Steven Spielberg, 1997) become inverted as humans occupy the position of unwanted invading aliens and the Na'vi are hopelessly besieged, pitted against a superior enemy and forced to fight back.

12 See Sigmund Freud, *The Interpretation of Dreams*, trans. and ed. James Strachey (New York: Penguin Books, 1984).

13 Ghassan Kanafani, "Returning to Haifa," in *Palestine's Children: Returning to Haifa and Other Stories*, trans. Barbara Harlowe and Karen E. Riley (Boulder: Lynne Rienner, 2000), 166–167.

14 See Ellen Grabiner, Donald E. Palumbo, and C. W. Sullivan, *I See You: The Shifting Paradigms of James Cameron's Avatar* (Jefferson, NC: MacFarland, 2012).

15 Slavoj Žižek, "*Avatar*: Return of the Natives," *New Statesman* (March 4, 2010): http://www.newstatesman.com/film/2010/03/avatar-reality-love-couple-sex.

16 Mark Fischer, *Capitalist Realism: Is There No Alternative?* (Winchester, UK: Zero Books, 2009), 16.

17 Fore, "The Tracks of Sully's Tears: Disability in James Cameron's *Avatar*," http://www.ejumpcut.org/archive/jc53.2011/fore Avatar/.

18 Fore, "The Tracks of Sully's Tears: Disability in James Cameron's *Avatar*," http://www.ejumpcut.org/archive/jc53.2011/foreAvatar/.

19 In Hollywood, native presence almost always appears initially as traces of native violence. In *Dances with Wolves*, arrows first enunciate native presence in a land otherwise appearing uninhabited.

20 Elisa Narminio and Matthew Wilhelm Kapell, "Between *Aliens* and *Avatar*: Mapping the Shifting Terrain of the Struggle for Women's Rights," in *The Films of James Cameron: Critical Essays*, eds Matthew Wilhelm Kapell and Stephen McVeigh (Jefferson, NC: MacFarland, 2011), 159–160.

21 Bruce Robbins, "Soul Making: Gayatri Spivak on Upward Mobility," *Cultural Studies* 17.1 (2003), 17–18.

22 A beautiful though indirect exposition of this hypothesis can be found in W. H. Auden, "The Quest Hero," in *Tolkein and His Critics: Essays on J.R.R. Tolkien's The Lord of the Rings*, eds Neil D. Isaacs and Rose A. Zimbardo (Notre Dame, IN: Notre Dame University Press, 1968).

23 Kristen Whissel, "Tales of Upward Mobility: The New Verticality and Digital Special Effects," in *Film Theory and Criticism: Introductory Readings*, eds Leo Braudy and Marshall Cohen (Oxford: Oxford University Press, 2009), 834–835.

24 See Timothy Hampton, *Writing from History: The Rhetoric of Exemplarity in Renaissance Literature* (Ithaca: Cornell University Press, 1990).

25 Cameron stated in an interview that he wants to produce two sequels to create a "family epic" depicting the life of the extended family of Jake and Neytiri. See Nick Perry, "James Cameron Clears Up *Avatar* Sequel Rumor," *AP News* (December 16, 2013): http://www.huffingtonpost.com/2013/12/16/james-cameron-avatar-sequels_n_4452393.html.

26 Jacques Derrida, *Specters of Marx: The State of Debt, the Work of Mourning, and the New International*, trans. Peggy Kamuf (New York: Routledge, 1994), 6.

27 Lev Manovich, "What is Digital Cinema?," in *Critical Visions in Film Theory: Classic and Contemporary Readings*, eds Timothy Corrigan, Patricia White, and Meta Mazaj (Boston: Bedford, 2011), 1060.

28 See Ann Marie Fallon, *Global Crusoe: Comparative Literature, Postcolonial Theory and Transnational Aesthetics* (Burlington, VT: Ashgate, 2011).

29 Kimberly N. Rosenfeld, "*Terminator* to *Avatar:* A Postmodern Shift," : *Jump Cut* 52 (2010): http://www.ejumpcut.org/archive/jc52.2010/RosenfeldAvatar/.

30 Žižek, "*Avatar*: Return of the Natives," http://www.newstatesman.com/film/2010/03/avatar-reality-love-couple-sex.

31 Grabiner, Palumbo, and Sullivan, *I See You*, 1.

32 Rjurik Davidson, "*Avatar*: Evaluating Film in a World of its Own," *Screen Education* 57 (2010): http://search.informit.com.au/documentSummary;dn=903277215022255;res=IELHSS.

33 Davis, "Native Images," http://ejumpcut.org/currentissue/DavisCGI/index.html.

34 See Philip Rosen, "Change Mummified," in *Film Theory & Criticism: Introductory Readings*, eds Leo Braudy and Marshall Cohen (Oxford: Oxford University Press, 2009), 822.

35 See Thomas Babington Macaulay, "Indian Education, The Minute of the 2nd of February, 1835," in *Macaulay: Prose and Poetry*, ed. G. M. Young (London: Rupert-Hart Davis, 1952).

36 Davis, "Native Images," http://ejumpcut.org/currentissue/DavisCGI/index.html.

37 See also Timothy Morton, *Ecology Without Nature*: *Rethinking Environmental Aesthetics* (Cambridge: Harvard University Press, 2007).

38 See Lata Mani, *Contentious Traditions: The Debate on Sati in Colonial India* (Berkeley: University of California Press, 1998).

39 The scene also appears in Mira Nair's 2012 film adaptation of Hamid's novel but with far less affect. While in the novel Erika almost forces Changez to play the role of Chris, the film treats the performance more as sexual play.

40 Ridley Scott's *Black Hawk Down* (2001) also focuses on the failure of the technocractic military gaze. US troops in the film fail to effectively control the site of invasion, as indigenous forces creep out firing from interstitial spaces causing serious damage to what was a meticulously planned extraction operation.

41 Andrew B. R. Elliot, "'She's a goddamn liar': Perspectives on Truth in *Aliens* and *Titanic*," in *The Films of James Cameron: Critical Essays*, eds Matthew Wilhelm Kapell and Stephen

McVeigh (Jefferson, NC: MacFarland, 2011), 83. See also Ace G. Pilkington, "Fighting the History Wars on the Big Screen: From *The Terminator* to *Avatar*," in *The Films of James Cameron: Critical Essays*, eds Matthew Wilhelm Kapell and Stephen McVeigh (Jefferson, NC: MacFarland, 2011), 44–71.

42 See Jolie Lee, "Giant Portrait in Pakistan gives Face to Drone Victims," *USA Today* (April 22, 2014): http://www.usatoday.com/story/news/nation-now/2014/04/22/not-a-bug-splat-pakistan-drones/7731325/.

43 Todd McGowan, "Looking for the Gaze: Lacanian Film Theory and its Vicissitudes," *Cinema Journal* 42 (2003), 29.

44 See Bron Taylor, "Prologue: *Avatar* as Rorschach," in *Avatar and Nature Spirituality*, ed. Bron Taylor (Waterloo, CA: Wilfrid Laurier University Press, 2013), 3–12; and Bron Taylor, "Epilogue: Truth and Fiction in *Avatar's* Cosmogony and Nature Religion," in *Avatar and Nature Spirituality*, ed. Bron Taylor (Waterloo, CA: Wilfrid Laurier University Press, 2013), 301–336.

45 Homi Bhabha, "Framing Fanon," Foreword to Frantz Fanon, *The Wretched of the Earth*, trans. Richard Philcox (New York: Grove Press, 2004), x.

46 James Cameron, quoted in Lisa Fitzpatrick, ed., *The Art of Avatar: James Cameron's Epic Adventure* (New York: Abrams, 2009), 7.

47 Gayatri Chakravorty Spivak, quoted in Robert Young, "Neocolonialism and the Secret Agent of Knowledge: An Interview with Gayatri Chakravorty Spivak," *Oxford Literary Review* 13.1 (July 1991): http://www.euppublishing.com/doi/abs/10.3366/olr.1991.010.

48 James Cameron, "A Message from Pandora": http://messagefrompandora.org/.

49 James Cameron, quoted in "Interview with Marguerite Suozzi: It's a Complete Reboot of how We See Things," *IPS News* (April 27, 2014): http://www.ipsnews.net/2010/04/qa-its-a-complete-reboot-of-how-we-see-things/.

50 James Cameron, quoted in "*Avatar* Director James Cameron Follows Box Office Success with Advocacy for Indigenous Struggles," *Democracy Now!* (April 27, 2010): http://www.

democracynow.org/2010/4/27/avatar_director_james_cameron_follows_box.

51 See Katherine Hayles, *How We Became Posthuman: Virtual Bodies in Cybernetics, Literature, and Informatics* (Chicago: University of Chicago Press, 1999).

Conclusion

The united symptoms of the West

This conclusion discusses two texts—one literary and one cinematic—that interrupt the West's continuing rehearsals of authorial privilege and subjective entitlement. Mahasweta Devi's Bengali short story "Sishu" or "Strange Children" (1989) and Michael Haneke's 2005 film *Caché* eviscerate the West's self-serving platitudes about the historically victimized Other.[1] Both Devi's story and Haneke's film can be read as critiques of such habitual Western imaginations, and as such are useful for the purpose of comparative reading against Cameron's film. In contrast to Cameron's narrative of subject-making, these texts violently disrupt the production of meaning, subjectivity, and audience satisfaction. These examples expose the seams of the West's unending imaginative vacuity about otherness and the substitution of otherness with fetishized images of the Other that serve the West's repeated need for performing its subjective reconstitution. Haneke and Devi's texts display alternative possibilities of representation—that is, representation not complicit with the production of absolute subjectivities. More specifically, a savage overflow of surplus meaning stalls the mechanisms of knowledge-production and subject formation in Devi's story and Haneke's film. Both narratives express what it entails to be truly imagined by other worlds—what it means to develop recognition of the other as constitutive of subjective identity and what happens to absolute subjectivities when the other speaks (back)!

Teleopoeisis and the predicament of the liberal subject

Cameron's film aligns with a particular tradition of Western imperialist thinking about the Other. This tradition involves repeated attempts at responsible engagements with the Other and it includes texts as diverse as Joseph Conrad's novella *The Heart of Darkness* (1899), Julia Kristeva's cultural study *About Chinese Women* (1977), Katherine Bigelow's film *The Hurt Locker* (2008), and Katherine Boo's popular nonfiction *Behind the Beautiful Forevers* (2012). The texts of this tradition conventionally describe literal and metaphoric journeys into the recesses of the Other and Europe's encounters with the inscrutable otherness of the Other. Barring a few instances such as those found in Claude Lévi-Strauss's *Triste tropiques* (1955), where the subject of Europe on confronting radical otherness realizes with utmost shock the failure of European knowledge systems, the narratives of this tradition mostly function to reassert Western sovereignty under the guise of understanding the Other. As Spivak puts it in an astute observation on French feminism (and Kristeva's text more specifically), "In spite of their occasional interest in touching the *other* of the West . . . their repeated question is obsessively self-centered: if we are not what official history and philosophy say we are, who then are we (not), how are we (not)?"[2]

According to Spivak, only a journey undertaken without apprehensions of or fears for possibility of radical self-dislocation can alone constitute a first step toward ethically engaging with the other. Spivak has a term for this act: teleopoeisis. Teleopoeisis is the exercise of stepping into the other's space and of being reimagined by the other, alien culture. Yet it is not easy to imagine the self through the desire of the other because this returns to the self the crippling fact of the subject's own being outside of itself—its excentricity. As such, it is not uncommon for cultural texts such as Cameron's *Avatar* to avoid this scenario altogether. And on the rare occasion that a text commits its protagonist to the scene of the other's desire and the intimate yet inaccessible alterity of the other, the structural dynamics of the scene typically substitutes the other's desire with the fantasy of the subject. One must remain with the desire of the subaltern other and experience its violent disturbance. But this truth often lies conveniently foreclosed in cultural discourses.

To see the difference between substituting a Western fantasy for the desire of the subaltern other and engaging with this desire, we can compare *Avatar* to *Sishu* and *Caché*. A postcolonial analysis of these texts, when read in context of my discussion of Cameron's film in the preceding chapter, will make clear the three differential possibilities involved in imagining the self: first, at the expense of the other (*Avatar*); second, in imagining the self via the other's desire (*Sishu*); and, finally, in resisting such imaginations *tout court* (*Caché*).

Let me begin by tracing the trajectory of the journey into otherness in two popular Western texts, namely Conrad's novella and Cameron's film. The *Heart of Darkness* and *Avatar* show liberal white heroes embarking on voyages into dark unknown spaces. Both heroes note with acute sensitivity the plight of the oppressed other, and both narratives fail correspondingly to complete their respective narrative-conceptual circuits. That is to say, the texts begin with a stated goal—to critique the naked and the guise of the West's imperial expansionism—yet both stop constitutively short of allowing their protagonists (and the audiences) any chance of being reimagined by the other's culture. The journeys in Conrad and Cameron's narratives enact habitual rhetorical excisions of the other, the fetishization of the Other, and the circumscription of the other in a moralist-humanist universe of European provenance. In this they are not unlike more direct articulations of Eurocentrism and racism. Overt Eurocentrism and blatant racism rely on precisely the same rhetorical strategies for debasing the other.

There are many critics who defend both texts as critiques of imperialism and colonialism rather than reading these as racist fantasies. This is more so in the case of *Avatar*. For instance, Cameron's hero, Sully, respects the Na'vi and painstakingly learns from them. And it is only after he finishes his lessons and successfully completes a series of tests that the Na'vi allow him into their tribe. In this way, Sully appears very different from the cold, dehumanizing perspectives of the natives evinced by Conrad's Kurtz and Marlowe. I have already disclosed the insincerity of the film's political gestures in the previous chapter. To repeat: *Avatar's* political correctness is the sign under which unfolds the ideological appropriation of the real other. The difference between Conrad's text and Cameron's film is one of degree—which of the two better mystifies the narrative use of the contingent Other as a prop for aiding the essential task of subject-production. Separated by exactly a hundred and ten years, Cameron's film is a rewriting or reimagination or incarnation of Conrad's novella for the twenty-first century. Both narratives record the age-old story of European subjective entitlement.

What could it mean, then, to be imagined by other worlds? With this question in mind let me turn to the texts of Devi and Haneke as texts interruptive of the tradition of European cultural imagination, knowledge-production, and subject formation.

An encounter with the radical otherness of the Other can only mean one thing: a complete disaster. A real encounter with a speaking subaltern heralds a complete breakdown of cognition, the State, and the Enlightenment Man. Such an event brings the divine closer to the mortal and the heaven nearer to earth, uprooting the thingness of the Other into a haunting apparition of otherness. In speaking, the other steps out of its consigned status as a fetish object to display its condition of a life as bereft of the most common social entitlements. Its appearance in this form violently rearranges matters of concern in excess of facts and history, and it also strips bare the outer face of humanity to reveal it as incorrigibly inhuman. The other's speech ushers in a new eloquence that forces recharacterization of being and exposes intersubjective relations as fragile and volatile.

Devi's story follows the trajectory of Conrad's novella and Cameron's film up to a point. Like these narratives, it too depicts the story of a man's journey into, and his experience of the Other's radical otherness. Haneke's film does not involve any literal journey into otherness, though the experiences of its central protagonist, a middle-class Parisian who hosts a literary review show on national television metaphorically indicate a journey into the space and time of the other. Devi's story, read as a text of minority literature alongside the Eurocentric tradition, and Haneke's film, analyzed in the context of audience expectations of popular Hollywood genres such as the film noir or the thriller, pose an interesting couple. They both exemplify what Will Higbee calls the *politics of transvergence*. That is, they both disrupt habits of meaning-making through the drastic foregrounding of traumatic otherness otherwise expunged from dominant narratives about the Other.[3]

A quick note: In reading a film alongside a literary text I wish to highlight the purchase of postcolonial theory as it cuts through and negotiates different representational mediums. Put differently, I wish to illustrate through my readings below that while postcolonial theory needs to adopt a set of different analytical tools and vocabulary for critically examining films, we do not need to overhaul its fundamental theoretical lenses of interrogation when moving from literature to film or film to literature. Postcolonial theory, whether employed to analyze a film or a short story, must remain acutely aware of the mechanism of subject-production, knowledge making, and the framing of otherness through foreclosure, disavowal, and repression.

The unbearable rubbing of the Other

Sishu is the story of an upper-caste Indian Central Government officer appointed to oversee drought relief in a tribal area in the east of the country. Like Marlowe and Sully, the officer enters the other's space responsibly. He respects the indigenes and is keen to immerse himself in their service. He has a feeling of pity for the indigenes, on the one hand, and a sense of duty to the nation, on the other. He knows these people need aid and believes that the nation state possesses the moral rectitude to ensure that they receive it. The welfare state must take care of its citizens irrespective of their caste, creed, religious affiliation, or gender identities.

The officer's journey into this forgotten tribal area is also a passage into knowledge and self-discovery. On witnessing first-hand the impoverished condition of these tribals, he awakens into a new reality. The officer realizes that everything he knew about the Indian tribals was wrong. Their "naked, emaciated" bodies with "bellies swollen with worms and thick spleen" shattered the romantic "images of tribal life" that he had "drawn from the movies."[4] This breakdown of the officer's imaginary knowledge about the indigene receives an immediate compensation with his ineluctable belief in the welfare nation state. Yet his faith in the state suffers a setback when he learns about an infamous incident involving the indigenes of the area and the government. He learns that some years previously, following the government's efforts to acquire tribal land for industry, a confrontation had ensued between some of the indigenes and the government. This led to the indigenes massacring government officials and then severe government retribution. In the most unfortunate turn of events, an entire tribal village went missing in the wake of the reprisals by the government forces. No one has since heard about the fate of these missing villagers.

Though disturbed by this information, the official has to focus on his job. He needs to ensure timely distribution of relief supplies. The greatest challenge he faces in this task is that of stolen supplies. Prior to his arrival, other government officials had forewarned him about the indigenes, saying that they were thieves by birth, stealing relief supplies and selling these in the black market for a profit. Other sources informed him about strange-shaped little children who purportedly stole the supplies in the dead of the night. Determined not to believe in such local lore and unfounded rumors about abnormal looking children, the officer decides to stay awake at nights and capture the thieves red-handed. One fateful night he hears scurrying footsteps and sets out to investigate. Very soon he stands face to face with these rumored apparitions—the "strange children." On getting closer though he realizes that these were not children but adults whose bodies had shrunk for some reason. The apparitions tell him that they are the very men and women charged of murdering the government officials and who, afraid of state reprisal, had disappeared years ago into the impenetrable jungles of the region. Surviving all these years on a frugal diet of leaves and roots, their bodies have shrunk, giving them a grotesque childlike form yet still appended with "dry and repulsive" adult genitals. These they rub against the body of the healthy relief officer as they slowly encircle him to tell their tale: "We're down to just these fourteen. Our bodies have shrunk. The men can't do anything with it except piss. The women can't get pregnant. That's why we steal food. We must eat to grow bigger again . . . We're like this because of the massacre of Kuva." Accosted by such "unbearable rubbing" of the other—an Other reduced to its most radical traumatic alterity—the officer is left questioning the reality of the "Copernican system, science, the twentieth century, the Independence of India, the five-year plans, all that he had known to be true." The story ends with him unable to bear the trauma: he decides to let out a scream to expel the horrific visions yet he cannot "make his voice scream." His speech dries up in face of the real. The officer turns into one who can no longer speak.[5]

At first glance, the similarities with and divergences from Cameron's film are easy to see. Conscientious individuals from the center embark on life-changing journeys into the heart of darkness with dreams that are soon shattered and substituted by a condemnation for the center. But the ending of the two stories are radically different, as the relief officer in Devi's story moves into a state of psychosis while Sully manages to save the indigene and live with them as a king. There is no rescue of the collapsed fantasy in Devi's work. Instead, an element of discord is introduced and left unresolved. This discord emerges as a site of resistance to hegemony not through the officer's failure to communicate or the subaltern's demand for justice but rather as an affect resulting from the unbearable rubbing of the Other's withered genitals on the body of the officer. The rubbed body of the officer symbolically represents the imaginary body politic of the inclusive decolonial nation state which is suddenly suspended in the scandalous desire of the subaltern's enjoyment.

The subaltern speaks in this story through a grotesque act of rubbing and displaying their genitalia. They assert their need to reproduce as more critical than their symbolic desire for remaining connected to their land, jungles, and hills. It is a need for survival. This articulation of a need to survive reveals the implicit systemic genocide of the indigenes—that is, the government's control of their bodies through exercising regulation over all aspects of their life and livelihood. The officer's encounter with the other opens to scrutiny the symbolic foundations of the imaginary community of the nation state; the fact of its independence and constitutional government come up short in the face of this traumatic experience. Yet we ought to be cautious about hastily identifying the speech of the other as adequately responding to years of silencing by the mainstream. On closer inspection, the story gives the final words to the agent of the state. Even though the officer cannot speak in the face of speech, the speech of the state reemerges within this scene of subaltern desire through the officer's remembering of five hundred years of South Asian history. His recollection of postcolonial Indian history interspersed with a history of enlightenment modernity segues into reassembling the identity of an average postcolonial Indian against that of the West. The officer thinks to himself why the indigenes target him, an "ordinary Indian." He ponders why he is "accused of a crime on behalf of all the others"? He compares himself almost instinctively with the Americans, the Canadians, and the Russians, who are all bigger in size than he and who eat more nutritious food than he ever has. This recalibration of postcolonial subjectivity via a politics of identifying the West as a realm of plenitude reproduces the chain of signification first introduced into the South Asian consciousness by colonialism and in the postcolonial context it aids the process of making meaning out of the subaltern's desire. Reframed by this repositioning of postcolonial subjectivity, the unpredictability and asymmetry of subaltern desires get folded into yet another sanitized universal fiction about identity formation in the decolonial world.

In the final analysis, postcolonial identity is positioned in contrast to the identity of the West. This expunges the heterogeneity of the decolonized nation state and the politics of what Spivak terms a negotiated independence. Within this reframing of national subjectivity the voice of the subaltern is once more expelled from the axiomatic structures of nationalist and decolonial histories of the sovereign nation state. Postcolonial theory should always remain suspicious of attempts to disengage marginality from particularity and its folding into consumable fictions of universality. Cameron's film and Devi's story thus begin with similar premises, and then part ways, but unfortunately converge again in their respective, albeit differential, treatments of radical otherness as an object of political sublime and what Ned O'Gorman calls "secular political piety."[6] The figures of the other in both texts are emptied of all particularity to support the fantasy of the dominant subject of history.

I began with Devi's story deliberately. I wished to start with a tempting promise of finding an alternative to Cameron's text and, eventually, to scuttle the associated expectation that such possible alternatives can be found only in Third World, postcolonial texts. The thinking that expects answers to be available in their texts—non-European texts—is precisely the kind of mindset that postcolonial theory sets out to dismantle. The Other is not in possession of a magical antidote to the West's ineluctable relationship with an array of misguided imperialist temperaments. As we see, Devi's story disrupts hegemonic fantasies but only to an extent. It successfully introduces the real conditions suffered by the South Asian indigene in symbolic terms. Similar to the politics of Fernando Birri (cinema and underdevelopment) and Glauber Rocha (aesthetics of hunger), Devi's text rescues the subaltern from representations of symmetric reality, romanticized Others, healthy bodies, and choreographed desires. Her narrative seeks to uncover a cached or hidden part of reality to comprehensively overturn reality itself. But ultimately the story fails. It reinscribes the desire of the sovereign state onto the scene of subaltern desire through a rememorialization of history as linear and universal and causal.

Within the chain of causality of this rememorialization, Copernican science leads to modern science and to the twenty-first century, and all of these in turn usher the decolonial national aftermath, but the presence of the subaltern as an unreadable signature within this symbolic matrix and as a surplus other resistant to the process of historical signification is effaced. By comparison, *Caché* offers a more stimulating narrative of transvergence. If Devi's story advances the narrative-conceptual circuit of teleopoeisis to some degree, then Haneke's film manages to capture successfully the logic of transvergence. While not embarking on any real or physical journey into the location of otherness, *Caché* ambitiously resists the hegemony of Western signification.

Caché or the intimate enemy

Caché is an allegory on the post-9/11 world. Haneke has himself stated in interviews that the film exceeds the Algeria–France colonial context that it explicitly addresses; instead, it is metaphoric of the dark underbelly of our twenty-first-century societies and our individual and collective culpability for the existence of these foreboding worlds. In "every country, there are dark corners—dark stains where questions of collective guilt become important," explains Haneke in one interview.[7] It is imperative to understand this metaphoric darkness in terms of affective memory and material effects produced by Europe's expansionist history. At the same time, the beauty of the film lies in its reluctance to be interpretatively mapped and historically ascertained. *Caché* renders audience expectations, the conventions of film genres, and critical interpretations, uncanny.

The film depicts a Parisian couple receiving packages containing video recordings of their home. Sometimes these recordings include drawings, disturbing sketches of a chicken being hacked by a child, whose meaning appear uncertain to most, except for Georges Laurent (Daniel Auteuil), the father to a twelve-year-old Pierrot (Lester Makedonsky) and husband to the affable Anne Laurent (Juliet Binoche). Georges withholds within him a dark, forgotten secret. The recordings and the drawings force Georges to remember his childhood and the secret that he had conveniently forgotten. Georges' personal and professional life is severely crippled as a direct consequence of receiving these uncanny tapes and strange drawings. He embarks therefore on a journey into remembering the past through his memories as well as a journey in the present to find the origin of the tapes. These excursions gradually take Georges as well as the audiences to the apartment of Majid (Maurice Bénichou). Majid's parents were Algerian immigrants who worked at Georges' family home but were killed in the Paris Massacre of 1961 at the height of the Algerian war for national independence. The orphaned Majid remained with Georges' family, but his growing proximity to the family made a young Georges uneasy. It is not clear in the film what really happens, though it seems that Georges could have tricked Majid into cutting the head off a rooster, and then promptly told his parents about Majid's heinous act, or he complained generally about Majid butchering chickens. In any case, we see Majid being eventually sent away against his will to an orphanage. Decades later, Georges becomes convinced that Majid is responsible for sending the tapes and sketches. But when

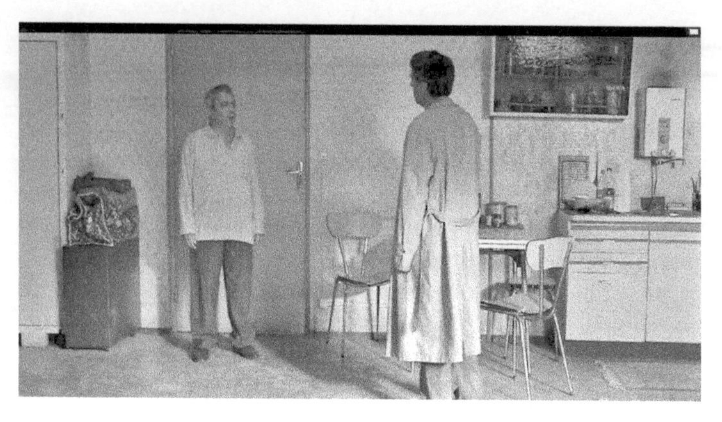

FIGURE 8 *Georges meets Majid (*Caché, *2005)*

Georges tracks Majid down and confronts him about the issue, the latter denies any knowledge. The meeting with Majid also unnerves Georges; memories of his childhood betrayal start to haunt him through dreams and nightmares.

Scenes in the film showing Georges' meetings with Majid encapsulate the dynamism of encountering the scene of the other's desire. It must be kept in mind that the other's articulation of desire does not automatically apprehend the subject in the other or otherness. Rather, such enunciations can construct a frame for our subjective being and offer, as Spivak puts it, "our so-called selves to ourselves," which we witness in Devi's story.[8] However, unlike in Devi's story, in Haneke's film there is no active mediation of the trauma of apprehending the self as an object in the other scene. Two crucial things happen in *Caché*. First, after the police harass Majid following Georges' complaint that Majid has kidnapped Pierrot, Majid invites Georges over to his rundown apartment to talk things over. Expecting Majid to confess about the tapes, Georges reluctantly agrees to the meeting. But Majid again denies any wrongdoing and then calmly slashes his own throat as a bewildered Georges looks on in horror. The suddenness with which Majid commits suicide is visually disarming for audiences as well. In this context, some critics have expressed shock while others have read the scene as typifying Haneke's style of violent filmmaking. But Majid's suicide and the velocity at which the act unfolds on the screen are apt in relation to Georges' encounter with the other. Majid speaks but Georges does not listen. He remains convinced of Majid's culpability. Perhaps realizing the only way to exorcize the specter haunting Georges requires the complete abstraction of himself from the scene, Majid kills himself. But does his death calm Georges' anxieties? At one level, by showing Georges retiring at the end of the film to his "padded bourgeois cocoon," Haneke seems to say yes.[9] But this scene appears to hold a false promise for Georges and the audiences of the film because a lingering final shot shows Majid's son and Pierrot conferring in front of the latter's school. This is the second crucial aspect. The certainty of bourgeois security that is established through the radical trauma of Majid's sudden suicide becomes craftily dismantled in the final shot. But in order to understand this final shot, one must look at it in context of the film's opening shot. The comparison reveals the overall narrative trajectory of the film.

The opening shot lingers like the final shot. It lasts for almost three minutes. Initially with the titles overlaid, it appears as an establishing shot but soon transforms into a disconcerting disembodied look. It takes a while though for audiences to realize that far from being an establishing shot cast from the director's camera, it is a film that has been shot by an anonymous person or persons, and, furthermore, the point of view for the shot is not the point of view of the anonymous person(s) but rather that of Georges and Anne who are watching the tape on their television. This series of dislocations fuel audience mistrust in the onscreen reality and disrupt genre expectations. For unlike the typical evil eye point of view of the film noir, Haneke never identifies the point of view in *Caché* as evil. The opening surveillance shot is actually an establishing shot in another sense of the term. Rather than establishing the location and thereby grounding the spectator's look, it establishes the spectator's position as fragile, indeterminate, and beyond individual control. It estranges the viewer from the enjoyment promised by cinema conceived as entertainment and the contentment of consumer satisfaction commonly offered by Hollywood productions such as *Avatar*. Instead this shot (as well as the final one) puts the audience, the critics, and the characters in the film in a state of parallel predicament with no idea about the origin of the gaze. This gaze leads all three into the domain of what Homi Bhabha terms the non-sense or, what Jacques Lacan once dubbed as, the slit in the symbolic present. Inhabiting this space, a subject is caught between seeing and not understanding, and is therefore forced to embark on a journey of self-discovery through contemplation of complicity, guilt, and responsibility in the face of the quandary she finds herself in. Like the officer in Devi's story the subject can, in a situation like this, recollect her being into historical re-existence, or, worse, like Cameron's hero, she can reconstitute subjectivity by framing the self through the logic of not knowing as a condition of becoming. Georges follows the footsteps of Devi's officer. He promptly imagines an Other and then personifies this Other as Majid. But this is not a simple gesture of othering the Other but rather one of connecting the associative links of an elaborate chain of signification that situates Georges and Majid's relationship at the axes of colonial history, decolonial politics, and social psychology all entangled in an unholy wedlock with capitalism. In the presence of the gaze and without this symbolization, the narrative as well as Georges risks growing intensely psychotic. Identifying Majid as his intimate enemy helps Georges to make sense of the strange epistles: he explains to himself that Majid wants revenge, or, better still, "Majid, an Algerian Muslim immigrant, who is my foster-brother, wants to kill me and destroy my family after all these years because as a child I had made a mistake!" Majid's suicide, however traumatic, comes as a welcome relief to Georges. Without the threatening presence of Majid—the neighbor, the foster-brother, the enemy within, and a colonial cousin—Georges can now sleep in peace.

Yet the promise of sleep proves short-lived as the final shot resurrects the specter of the disembodied gaze. This lingering shot unravels the chain of signification constructed by Georges. It frustrates Georges' ability to control knowledge in order to recompose his subjectivity and reinscribes the uncertainty and feeling of alienation experienced at the opening scene back into the cinematic space. As critics and audiences continue to struggle trying to decide whether this shot shows the return of the disembodied gaze encountered at the opening of the film or whether this scene comes from the point of view of the director's camera that gives audiences a glimpse of what was going on after all—namely, Pierrot along with Majid's son sent the tapes—*Caché* returns us to the liminal, the non-sense, the split.[10] Whether we conceive this space of uncertainty after Spivak as a limit to exercises of meaning-making or after Lacan as a pulsation that loops through life without any particular goal or purpose, the absence of closure in *Caché* makes it a postcolonial film. It contrasts with Cameron's film and its ideology of subject formation by showing the impossibility of any meaning-making exercise within the space–time continuum we identify as the social present. It is not that it is impossible to make sense of Haneke's film. But our efforts to make sense of it can only lead us toward abstractions such as God or allegorical referents in history.[11] Meaning as pure signification is impossible just as subject formation cannot be free from practices of objectification of the other.

Caché is pivotal to reimagining postcolonial theory in the globalized present. Like postcolonial theory, it teaches us to be unconditionally suspicious of all forms and modes of cultural production of meaning. Better still, it counts itself in that process of inquiry and introspection. If it evokes in audiences the condition of being reimagined by an other (another gaze), then it also repeatedly scuttles its own narrative efforts at overwriting the place of non-meaning with meaning. *Caché* rehearses the contemporaneous ways in which we seek to design knowledge as universal and like to imagine our subjectivity as liberal-multicultural in order to demonstrate the sheer hypocrisy of these endeavors. It reveals knowledge as incommensurable with and subjectivity as irreconcilable with the other. Our recent exercises toward establishing solidarity among humans of all orders of life and even across species boundaries betray the same logic that galvanized colonial discourses of the previous three centuries.

Notes

1 See Mahasweta Devi, *"Sishu" [Strange Children] of Women, Outcastes, Peasants, and Rebels*, trans. Kalpana Bardhan (Berkeley, Los Angeles and Oxford: University of California Press, 1990).

2 Gayatri Chakravorty Spivak, *In Other Worlds* (New York: Routledge, 1998), 188–189.

3 See Will Higbee, "Beyond the (trans)national: Towards a Cinema of Transvergence in Postcolonial and Diasporic Francophone Cinema(s)," *Studies in French Cinema* 7.2 (2007): 79–91.

4 Devi, "Strange Children," 230. The temptation to romanticize the tribal other is quite strong. Even a director of Satyajit Ray's stature fall victim to this impulse. In his last film, *Aguntuk* [The Stranger] (1991), Ray constitutes indigenous populations of the globe as one unit, existing on the margins of bourgeois societies as examples of alternative communities, versed in herbal medicine, and in close connection to nature. The tribal as an outside—with a nostalgic lost history and closed to mainstream domains of existence—functions in this film just as it does elsewhere including Cameron's *Avatar* to self-reflectively criticize bourgeois social mores and moral values in order to reinvent the bourgeois subjectivity as more open to these others; more sympathetic, more charitable, more liberal.

5 Devi, "Strange Children," 240–241.

6 Ned O'Gorman, "The Political Sublime: An Oxymoron," *Millennium – Journal of International Studies* 34 (2006): 889–890.

7 Michael Haneke, quoted in Richard Porton, "Collective Guilt and Individual Responsibility: An Interview with Michael Haneke," *Cineaste* (Winter 2005): 50–51.

8 Gayatri Chakravorty Spivak, *Outside the Teaching Machine* (New York: Routledge, 1993), 159.

9 L. Saxton, "Secrets and Revelations: Off-screen Space in Michael Haneke's *Caché* (2005)," *Studies in French Cinema* 7.1 (2007): 10.

10 Haneke does not make matters easy. Pursuant to his politics of frustrating audience expectations for "Cinderella endings" to films, he dismisses the idea that Pierrot plotted with Majid's son or that the shot showing the two meeting has any resolute connotation. See, M. Haneke and S. Toubiana, Interview on *Caché* (DVD, Les Films du Losange, 2005); and Scott Foundas, "Interview: Michael Haneke: The Bearded Prophet of *Code Inconnu* and *The Piano Teacher*," (2001): http://www.indiewire.com/people/int_Haneke_Michael_011204.html.

11 G. Mecchia, "The Children Are Still Watching Us, *Caché*/Hidden in the folds of Time," *Studies in French Cinema* 7.2 (2007): 132.

FURTHER READING

(From the easiest to the most difficult):

1. Aimé Césaire, *Discourse on Colonialism*, trans. Joan Pinkham (New York: Monthly Review Press, 2000). This poetic critique of imperialism echoes points made by Fanon regarding the dehumanization of Man in colonialism, the loss of native culture and identity, and the culturalization of colonial politics. It then extends to identify the rise of Fascism in Europe as resulting from Europe's territorial aspirations and forcible occupation of lands. This is a must read for all students of colonial and postcolonial cultures.
2. Samir Amin, *Eurocentrism*, trans. Russell Moore (New York: Monthly Review Press, 1989). Amin explains Eurocentrism as a mindset that germinates fully in post-Enlightenment Europe. *Eurocentrism* is not just descriptive of Western prejudices about and inaccuracies in representations of the non-European Other but rather an explication of the assumption that different cultures shape different historical paths for its respective cultural inhabitants. Students will find this book useful to understanding the phenomenon of Eurocentrism.
3. Ania Loomba, *Colonialism/Postcolonialism* (New York: Routledge, 1998). This book offers an accessible introduction to postcolonial studies. The author begins by considering the etymology of the term "colonia" and ends with a discussion of the relevance of postcolonial studies in the era of globalization. The book contains useful examples of the use of postcolonial theory for cultural analysis.
4. Leela Gandhi, *Postcolonial Theory: A Critical Introduction* (New York: Columbia University Press, 1998). This book offers a useful introduction to postcolonial theory. It begins by overviewing the development of the methodology and the theoretical contours of the discipline through anti-colonial thinkers such as Mohandas

Gandhi and Frantz Fanon and runs through the works of Edward Said before ending with a discussion of the limits of postcolonial theory in the age of globalization.

5 Bill Ashcroft, Gareth Griffiths, and Helen Tiffin, eds, *The Post-colonial Studies Reader* (New York: Routledge, 1995), Or, Patrick Williams and Laura Chrisman, eds, *Colonial Discourse and Postcolonial Theory: A Reader* (New York: Columbia University Press, 1994). Both these edited collections bring together writings by some of the most influential postcolonial theorists of the last three decades and serve as the perfect sampler for students seeking to gain introduction to the main ideas of the field. Students will find both volumes indispensable as they acquaint themselves with the discipline.

6 Ella Shohat and Robert Stam, *Unthinking Eurocentrism: Multiculturalism and the Media* (New York: Routledge, 1994). This book introduces "multicultural media studies" as a methodology for critically examining the circulation of Eurocentrism in twenty-first-century popular media and postmodern cultures. Students will find the attempt of the authors to decouple multiculturalism as politics from the cultural absorption of multiculturalism in the rhetoric of liberal humanism extremely useful.

7 Ella Shohat and Robert Stam, eds, *Multiculturalism, Postcoloniality, and Transnational Media* (New Brunswick, NJ: Rutgers University Press, 2003). This collection of essays complements *Unthinking Eurocentrism* with a wide range of essays on an equally diverse collection of topics relating to multiculturalism, postcoloniality, and transnational media.

8 Michael Atkinson, ed., *Exile Cinema: Filmmakers at Work Beyond Hollywood* (Albany: State University Press, 2008). The essays in the book offer an excellent introduction to filmmakers outside Western Europe and the United States as well as those working on the fringes of mainstream filmmaking in Europe and the US. An important book for students wishing to expand their knowledge of films and filmmakers beyond Hollywood and Francois Truffaut, Akira Kurosawa, Andrei Tarkovosky, and Jean-Luc Godard.

9 Ania Loomba, Suvir Kaul, Matti Bunzl, Antoinette Burton, and Jed Esty, eds, *Postcolonial Studies and Beyond* (Durham: Duke

University Press, 2005). The essays in this collection come primarily from the "Postcolonial Studies and Beyond" conference held at the University of Illinois at Urbana-Champaign in 2002, and debates the status of postcolonial theory in the context of globalization and the emergence of the West as a technologized, networked, and juridical empire. This book will introduce students to the current debates around the discipline.

10 Sara Ahmed, *The Promise of Happiness* (Durham, NC: Duke University Press, 2010). Ahmed's theoretical exploration of what constitutes happiness is not film specific, but she uses many filmic instances including *Bend It Like Beckham* and *Children of Men* to explain her arguments. Of interest to students would be her analysis of films through a model that combines feminist, postcolonial, and queer theories with psychoanalysis and critical race studies.

11 Russell Fergusson, Martha Gever, Trinh T. Minh-ha, and Cornell West, eds, *Out There: Marginalization and Contemporary Cultures* (New York: New York Museum of Contemporary Art and Cambridge, MA: The MIT Press, 1990). This collection contains full-length essays by influential thinkers whose writings inform the theories and praxis of postcolonial theory, critical race studies, multicultural media studies, cultural politics, etc. Students wishing to explore more about how marginalization of different others unfold in the context of museum exhibits, photography, news coverage, and other forms of late twentieth century cultural expressions will find this book extremely useful.

12 Alain Grosrichard, *The Sultan's Court: European Fantasies of the East* (1979), trans. Liz Heron (New York: Verso, 1998). Published a year after Edward Said's *Orientalism*, Grosrichard's book is not as well known in the Anglo-American academy. It deals with the issue of Europe's fantasies about and anxieties over the figure of the Oriental despot. This book is useful for exploring the topic of subject-production and knowledge formation through the site of fantasy. One of the strongest suits of the book is its methodology: it uses Lacanian theory but this does not compromise its postcolonial focus in any way. The English translation carries an excellent introduction by Mladen Dolar titled "The Subject Supposed to Enjoy" which gives a

useful summary of Grosrichard's methodological and perspectival differences from Said.

13 Partha Chatterjee, "After Subaltern Studies," *Economic & Political Weekly*, XLVII, 35 (September 1, 2012): http://www.epw.in/perspectives/after-subaltern-studies.html. An extremely important essay penned by one of the leading figures of the subaltern studies field, this piece argues for reinventing subaltern studies in the wake of the death of postcolonial theory through engagements with popular culture, especially populist films.

14 Christopher Lane, ed., *The Psychoanalysis of Race* (New York: Columbia University Press, 1998). An excellent collection of essays that examine the applicability of psychoanalytic theory for understanding identity politics, race relations, imperialist discourses, and popular cinema.

15 Gayatri Chakravorty Spivak, "Introduction," in Jacques Derrida's *Of Grammatology*, trans. Gayatri Chakravorty Spivak (Baltimore: Johns Hopkins University Press, 1976). Though it does not teach film analysis, the introduction as an example of a self-reflexive postcolonial interrogation of European epistemologies and cultural production of meaning offers valuable lessons in pursuing theoretical analysis.

INDEX

www.ingramcontent.com/pod-product-compliance
Ingram Content Group UK Ltd.
Pitfield, Milton Keynes, MK11 3LW, UK
UKHW031250020325
455689UK00008B/105